MANAGING
CREDIT
DEPARTMENT
FUNCTIONS

A MANAGER'S GUIDE TO IMPROVING LOAN ANALYSIS, DOCUMENTATION AND REPORTING

KENNETH R. PIROK

A Bankline Publication

IRWIN
Professional Publishing

Chicago • Bogotá • Boston • Buenos Aires • Caracas
London • Madrid • Mexico City • Sydney • Toronto

A BankLine Publication

ISBN 1-55738-755-7

Printed in the United States of America

BB

1 2 3 4 5 6 7 8 9 0

JB

TABLE OF CONTENTS

LIST OF FIGURES

PREFACE

Managing Credit Department Functions is a reference manual useful to anyone involved in the operation of the credit department of a financial institution. The manual is intended for use by individuals involved in starting a new credit department or in improving existing commercial loan analysis or commercial loan administration functions.

The manual includes internal aspects of the Credit Department such as operations, communication, research, training, leadership, and motivation. For this reason, it is an essential reference for the credit department manager. In addition, the manual addresses credit department structuring, staffing, and relationships with other departments as well as the importance of commercial loan analysis to the financial institution. It is, therefore, also important reading for the senior lender and the president as well as for administrators overseeing the lending and loan analysis functions. The manual even contains numerous ideas, sample forms, definitions, and information useful to credit department members such as credit analysts who wish to improve themselves or their department.

ACKNOWLEDGMENTS

The TurboFAST system was used to produce the computer spreadsheets in Chapter 2. TurboFAST is produced by Financial Proformas, Inc., 1855 Olympic Boulevard, Suite 200, Walnut Creek, California 94596.

The real estate appraisal review form in Chapter 8 was provided by Michael T. White.

INTRODUCTION

The credit department exists to support various bank goals and objectives. The typical credit department supports all or most of the following:

- Reduction of nonperforming or adversely rated loans

- Loan growth

- Improved organization

- Loan documentation

- Accurate decision making

- Accurate loan reporting

If your bank has not met its goals in these areas or if it wishes to improve itself in these areas, then it should create a credit department if it does not already have one, or it should reevaluate the existing credit department and attempt to improve its operation. This book is written for anyone involved in either creating a new credit department or in reevaluating an existing credit department.

Note that, as an alternative to "credit department," the commercial credit area is typically named "credit administration department" when its duties include loan administration and/or loan operations, and it is also frequently named "credit analysis department" or "commercial loan analysis department" if its operation is strictly limited to loan analysis.

In many aspects, the credit department and the management of the credit department is no different than the typical business operation. For example, the department should have a business plan. A business plan is an outline of the department's environment and its operations as well as goals and objectives to guide the department.

The first step in creating or evaluating the business plan is to create or to understand the credit department's mission. The mission simply and generally describes the department's primary goal or its primary function. Bank management has likely developed a formal mission statement for the entire bank. It is important for all department members to be familiar with the bank's mission. In addition, the credit department's own mission should be consistent with the bank's mission.

This book assumes that the primary activity of the credit department is commercial loan analysis. Credit department members, typically called credit analysts, perform various types of analysis used to make loan decisions. The analysis work product is presented to a loan officer or to a loan committee for use in an approval or denial decision, for a risk-rating decision, or for ongoing monitoring.

Credit analysis is essentially a control or an audit type of function. It exists so that an independent party, or a "devil's advocate," reviews commercial loan relationships. This is important since the loan officer, himself or herself, cannot be completely objective and may not have time to properly analyze his or her own clients. The ultimate responsibility of the credit department is, therefore, to provide objectively prepared information.

In addition to loan analysis, the credit department may be responsible for loan documentation or documentation review, preparation of economic or market research, preparation of loan quality, pricing, or board reports, assuring compliance with regulations, or for answering credit inquiries.

Additional commercial lending support activities may be mentioned in the mission if they are an integral part of credit department operations. The degree to which the credit department offers additional services to lenders is an important aspect of the department's business plan. In addition, it is important to realize that commercial lenders are the "customers" of the credit department.

A credit department mission statement might be, "The credit department provides accurate, timely, and objective commercial loan analysis to support loan decision making and monitoring." Or its mission could focus on service: "The credit department supports the commercial lending function. Department members provide financial statement spreadsheets, loan analysis, industry analysis, documentation review, and file maintenance, and complete various other projects as needed by the lending area."

In order to support the mission, specific goals should be set to guide the department. Goals are important because they provide specific details concerning what the department wishes to accomplish and because they guide department members in pursuit of these accomplishments. It is important that both credit department members and those who work with the credit department understand the goals. credit department goals might include:

- 100 percent accuracy and uniformity of spreads and commercial loan analysis;

- Five-day turnaround time for requests for loan analysis by officers; and/or

- 90 percent accuracy of proposed risk-ratings made by analysts.

Once goals have been set, the structure of the department can be addressed. Chapter 1, "How to Structure the Department," discusses the credit department's place in the bank as well as the staffing of the credit department.

After the planning and the staffing of the credit department are complete, it can begin to operate. Chapter 2, "How to Get Organized and Operate the Department," and Chapter 3, "Communication and Research," discuss both the operation of the department and the various sources of information available to the department.

Chapter 4, "Training," Chapter 5, "Leading and Motivating Department Members," and Chapter 6, "How to Institute an Incentive Program," discuss various ideas and strategies that the credit department manager can use to lead and to interact with the department members.

As the credit department personnel become experienced, further responsibility can be undertaken. Chapter 7, "Additional Services the Credit Department Can Offer," and Chapter 8, "Regulations and Compliance," discuss additional services that the department can perform and additional information with which the department can work.

Finally, the summary of the book details a typical commercial loan analysis process. Following the summary is a glossary of credit department and commercial lending terms.

SOURCE

Daft, Richard L. *Management.* (Chicago: The Dryden Press, 1988), 2–27, 98–126.

CHAPTER ONE

HOW TO STRUCTURE THE DEPARTMENT

INDEPENDENCE

The credit department should operate separately from the commercial lending department. Department members should not report to commercial lenders. Instead, the department manager or department members should report directly to the senior loan officer or to another bank administrator who is not responsible for maintaining commercial loan relationships.

Independence from commercial lending allows the credit department to maintain its objectivity. The credit department exists, in part, to find weaknesses in commercial loans. Therefore, a conflict of interest exists if department members report to someone whose responsibility it is to make loans.

Even when credit department members do not report to commercial lenders, it is important to remain objective. When a credit analyst or even the credit department manager wishes to become a commercial lender, he or she may be tempted to avoid presentation of unfavorable aspects of certain loans. This temptation results from the perception that such presentation will be displeasing to the Commercial Loan Department Manager or to the members of the commercial lending department and will harm one's chances for promotion. In reality, it is most likely that credit department members gain the most respect from commercial loan department members when all unfavorable aspects of loans are presented, as long as the presentation is accurate and diplomatic.

Further, the credit department should be allowed complete control over the content of its analysis product. Although suggestions and background from the loan officer are essential, a conflict of interest exists if the loan officer has the authority to edit the loan analysis.

Loan officer comments and reaction to loan analysis should, however, be encouraged. Loan officer comments should be included as an attachment to the analysis if he or she objects to any part of the analysis, or if he or she wishes to highlight any aspect of the analysis.

RELATIONSHIP WITH COMMERCIAL LENDERS

The credit department interacts with the commercial lending department on a daily basis, and the success of this relationship is crucial to the success of the credit department. A healthy relationship consists of a balancing act between mutual respect and understanding as well as a small degree of disagreement.

It is important to realize that there will be some degree of resistance from the commercial lending department when the credit department is started up or restructured. Lenders may feel as if some of their power is being taken from them. They may be resistant to allowing the credit department to perform such activities as preparing loan presentations, examining loan documents, making recommendations, and attending loan committee meetings or customer calls.

This reaction from the commercial lending department is natural. An excellent way to address the concerns of the lenders is to explain to them that the credit department exists to **support** the commercial lending function. The credit department will alleviate some of the stress and take over some of the tasks that lenders are required to perform. This will leave more time for sales activities.

Lenders may also be resistant because they are simply unfamiliar with some of the tasks and techniques of the credit department. Credit analysts are often the experts on accounting, financial statements, financial analysis, and cash flow. Care should be taken to explain or to clear up any aspects of a loan analysis that are unclear to the lender. This is important because the lender typically presents the loan to the committee using the analyst's loan presentation, and because the committee must understand the presentation in order to make a decision.

A series of short training sessions on how the credit department operates and how it analyzes loans can be performed soon after the department begins operation or is restructured. The training sessions are an excellent way to avoid future confusion and disagreement between the two departments. Training sessions and communication allow the two departments to know what to expect from each other.

While the relationship between the credit department and the commercial lending department should be one of mutual respect and understanding, it should actually include some degree of conflict as well. If the credit department and the commercial lending department seldom or never disagree on analysis results, then the credit department may not be performing its duty as a conservative, independent opinion, or as the "devil's advocate." It is perfectly normal and reasonable for disagreement to occur concerning proposed loan ratings, cash flow calculations, collateral valuations, and overall analysis results.

Commercial lenders are salespeople whose job is to make commercial loans. It is important not to be offended when a lender dislikes some aspect of a loan presentation prepared by the credit department. The lender is not attacking the analyst personally. Rather, he or she is attempting to argue in favor of his or her loan. If a disagreement cannot be resolved, then each side should realize and respect the fact that the other party is simply attempting to perform his or her job. A fair compromise is to present the analysis both ways, allowing the approving body to decide which is more appropriate.

Disagreement, along with discussion whereby each side presents an argument, is the very purpose for which the credit department exists. Discussion and disagreement are crucial elements of the loan decision process. They ensure that all drawbacks to a loan are considered before the loan is made. The result is a more accurate loan decision.

If the relationship between the credit department and the commercial lending department becomes strained, and if disagreement becomes frequent or uncontrollable, then measures should be taken to increase communication between the two departments. For example, new training sessions on analysis principles and/or loan policy will help both parties to use the same guidelines and assumptions. Further, instituting informal lunches or activities outside the bank can help improve rapport between credit analysts and commercial lenders. This is important since the credit department is a crucial part of the commercial loan approval process and since most credit analysts are future commercial lenders.

USE OF DEPARTMENT WORK

Commercial loan analysis is performed to benefit the bank. The goal of loan analysis is **not** satisfaction of regulators or internal loan review. Instead, analysis is used to support loan approval and risk rating decisions. Therefore, analysis that is seen only by the credit file and not by the loan officer or loan committee is a wasted analysis. Although it satisfies regulators, the analysis does no good for the bank.

It is difficult to force credit department analysis to be used for loan decisions since the loan decision makers are members of a separate department. However, methods do exist to promote effective use of the credit department's work product.

The department can track maturing notes on its own. Whenever a credit department analysis is required for renewal, the analysis can be presented to the loan officer before the renewal decision needs to be made. Such tracking is also a nice service to provide to the busy loan officer.

The department can also become responsible for distributing loan write-ups directly to loan committee members. This ensures that analysis performed by the credit department is presented to the loan committee whenever required by policy.

Department members can even become responsible for the production of loan committee minutes. This ensures that all loans approved according to the minutes have been analyzed and presented to the committee as required, and it also provides excellent experience to the department member who produces the minutes.

Whenever work is requested to be filed directly by the analyst when finished, it should be assigned the lowest priority. Unless the requesting loan officer will use this analysis for some purpose other than to pad the file, the analysis has very little value to the bank.

THE CREDIT DEPARTMENT'S ROLE IN THE BANK

To summarize, the credit department exists to support the commercial lending department and the loan decision-making process. To perform this role, the credit department must remain independent and objective while also remaining supportive and informative. The credit department should promote itself by proactively seeking analysis opportunities and by encouraging commercial lenders to use analysis effectively. The result will be more accurate loan decisions and greater feelings of importance by credit department members.

STAFFING

After the reasons for the existence of the credit department and its role within the bank are defined, the credit department can begin to be structured. The department must be staffed with enough people to be effective, and the choices of each staff member must be made with the department's goals, objectives, and needs in mind.

The credit department is typically staffed by recent college graduates. A college degree, specifically a degree in accounting, finance, or business administration, is a typical prerequisite. This requirement usually exists since the credit analyst must have a working knowledge of banking, accounting, real estate, insurance, finance, and management to be effective. A recent business school graduate, although inexperienced, typically has the knowledge and the motivation to perform successfully. In addition, an analyst hired directly from college has not developed philosophies that may differ from those of the bank; therefore, he or she can be trained easily.

Consideration should also be given to promotion from within when hiring credit analysts. Current bank employees from loan or deposit operations, from retail banking, or from the teller line frequently possess the educational qualifications necessary as well as enthusiasm toward the commercial lending area, which make them excellent candidates. In addition, such employees have practical banking knowledge and experience, which is extremely valuable.

The credit analyst position is usually considered to be an entry, level position into the commercial lending area. Turnover is frequent in the credit department since many analysts are promoted to commercial lending positions within the first few years of their employment. In addition to credit analyst positions, many credit departments employ a file clerk or someone who is solely responsible for tracking, spreading, and organizing financial statements. These positions provide support to the credit analysts and to the lenders, and they also provide experience for someone who wishes to become a credit analyst.

The size of the credit department depends on variables such as the size of the bank, the size of the commercial loan portfolio, the size of the loans that the department analyzes, and the types of services that the department offers. The author conducted a survey of 23 small and medium-sized banks to determine the general size of the credit department based on the dollar amount of total bank assets, the dollar amount of total commercial and commercial real estate loans, and the total number of commercial and commercial real estate accounts. (See Figure 1–1 at this end of the chapter.)

Based on the survey, the average credit department has one member for every $148,132,000 in total bank assets; one member for every $37,257,000 in commercial and commercial real estate loans; and one member for every 296 commercial and commercial real estate accounts. The results of the survey are quite variable. Total bank assets per credit department member ranged from $5 million to $500 million, and commercial loan amounts per department member ranged from $1 million to $100 million.

It is important to note that every credit department performs a different function. For example, in addition to credit analysts, it is likely that personnel performing loan operations, loan documentation, loan review, clerical support, and even lending are included in credit department sizes reported in the survey. At the same time, other banks surveyed employ and report only credit analysts as the total makeup of the credit department, while banks reporting zero credit department members require that loan officers perform loan analysis.

CREDIT DEPARTMENT JOB DESCRIPTIONS

The following credit department job descriptions provide a basis for the construction of specific job descriptions for your department members. The descriptions are general enough to be useful to a department comprised of only one or two members as well as to a department comprised of 20 members. The functional tasks in the job descriptions are discussed throughout the book.

Credit Department Assistant or Secretary or File/Note Clerk

Reports to:
- Credit Manager

Requirements:
- High-school diploma or equivalent
- Writing and verbal communication skills
- Advanced typing skills
- Organization skills

Activities:
- File documents.
- Keep files and notes organized
- Check files and notes in and out
- Request lien searches and title searches
- Request credit reports on loan applicants and borrowers
- Produce or assist in preparation of reports as required, such as commercial loan presentations, industry analyses, concentration of credit analysis, risk-rating reporting, and loan committee minutes
- Make copies and faxes of loan analysis projects and distribute them to loan committee members

Credit Analyst Trainee or Credit Analyst I

Reports to:
- Credit Manager

Requirements:
- College degree in business-related field or equivalent work experience
- Analytical skills
- Writing and verbal communication skills
- Basic typing skills

Activities:
- Spread financial statements.
- Work with commercial lenders and credit department members to produce cash flow analyses, collateral analyses, memoranda to officers, and formal, written loan presentations to analyze the ability of (basic or average) commercial borrowers to repay debt to the bank
- Produce reports as required, such as industry analyses, concentration of credit analysis, risk-rating reporting, and loan committee minutes

Credit Analyst II

Reports to:
- Credit Manager

Requirements:
- College degree in business-related field and/or 1–2 years commercial loan analysis experience
- Analytical skills
- Writing and verbal communication skills
- Basic typing skills
- Ability to provide leadership

Activities:
- Spread financial statements
- Work with commercial lenders and credit department members to produce cash flow analyses, collateral analyses, memoranda to officers, and formal, written loan presentations to analyze the ability of (most complex) commercial borrowers to repay debt to the bank
- Produce reports as required such as industry analyses, concentration of credit analysis, risk-rating reporting, and loan committee minutes.
- Provide leadership, support, assistance, and training to credit analyst trainees or credit analyst i's.
- Attend customer calls with Commercial Loan Officers

Credit Analyst III or Assistant Credit Manager or Senior Credit Analyst or Credit Officer

Reports to:
- Credit Manager

Requirements:
- College degree in business related field and/or significant commercial loan analysis experience

- Analytical skills
- Writing and verbal communication skills
- Basic typing skills
- Advanced leadership skills

Activities:
- Supervise credit department in the absence of the credit manager
- Work with commercial lenders and credit department members to produce cash flow analyses, memoranda to officers, and formal, written loan presentations to analyze the ability of (most complex) commercial borrowers to repay debt to the bank
- Produce reports as required such as industry analyses, concentration of credit analysis, risk-rating reporting, and loan committee minutes
- Provide leadership, support, assistance, and training to credit analyst trainees or credit analysts
- Attend customer calls with commercial loan officers.

The actual job descriptions used by your department will likely be more detailed than those presented here. Specific tasks performed by each member of your department can be detailed, and the job descriptions can be tailored to the people holding the positions or to the types of people for whom you are looking to hold certain positions.

Typical credit department members possess a wide range of talents, abilities, and job functions. For example, many of the more advanced credit analyst positions require leadership and teaching skills in addition to pure analytical skills required of new analysts. Job descriptions should reflect the need for these skills.

Job descriptions and job functions can also be tailored so that the needs of the department members are met. Some department members may desire positions as commercial lenders, while others may desire to remain in the credit department for their entire careers. A credit analyst desiring to become a lender should receive some exposure to customer calls, to the loan committee process, and to loan structuring and documentation while still an analyst. The job description can outline these functions.

Job descriptions are a useful tool to organize the initial credit department staffing and the ongoing staffing process. They provide a first step to outline what is needed and what is expected from department members. Job descriptions help fulfill the needs of the bank, the needs of the department, and even the needs of the department member.

FIGURE 1–1: STAFFING SURVEY

TOTAL BANK ASSET SIZE	TOTAL COMMERCIAL COMM. R.E. LOANS	TOTAL ACCOUNTS	ANALYSIS STAFF	ASSETS TO STAFF SIZE	LOANS TO STAFF SIZE	ACCOUNTS TO SIZE
$197,596,000	$85,739,000	809	3.0	$65,865,333	$28,579,666	270
$31,268,000	$5,294,000	244	2.5	$12,507,200	$2,117,600	98
$973,372,000	$316,853,000	N/A	17.5	$55,621,257	$18,105,886	N/A
$403,000,000	$118,000,000	1,025	2.0	$201,500M	$59,000,000	513
$61,372,000	$6,529,000	N/A	6.0	$10,228,667	$1,088,167	N/A
$1,388,667,000	$521,831,000	4,240	9.0	$154,296M	$57,981,222	471
$136,224,000	$60,429,000	494	1.0	$136,224M	$60,429,000	494
$358,700,000	$64,700,000	N/A	3.0	$119,567M	$21,566,667	N/A
$482,743,000	$123,385,000	N/A	12.0	$40,228,583	$10,282,083	N/A
$829,000,000	$120,000,000	N/A	7.5	$110,533M	$16,000,000	N/A
$20,865,000	$4,301,000	107	4.0	$5,216,256	$1,075,365	27
$6,400,368,000	$1,164,000,000	3,000	14.0	$457,169M	$83,142,857	214
$117,852,000	$67,351,000	N/A	1.25	$94,281,600	$53,880,800	N/A
$205,331,000	$49,750,000	291	1.5	$136,888M	$33,166,738	194
$2,900,000,000	$370,000,000	225	9.0	$322,222M	$41,111,111	25
$23,000,000	$10,000,000	N/A	0.0	N/A	N/A	N/A
$243,000,000	$51,000,000	N/A	0.5	$486,000M	$102,000M	N/A
$644,000,000	$150,000,000	N/A	7.0	$92,000,000	$21,428,571	N/A
$94,000,000	$51,000,000	N/A	0.0	N/A	N/A	N/A
$233,000,000	$94,000,000	N/A	2.0	$116,500M	$47,000,000	N/A
$531,000,000	$60,000,0000	N/A	2.0	$265,500M	$30,000,000	N/A
$854,891,000	$364,623,000	1,444	8.0	$106,861M	$45,577,875	181
$303,928,000	$122,134,000	1,923	2.5	$121,571M	$48,853,600	769
AVERAGE:						
$757,964,000	$173,083,000	1,255	5.0	$148,132M	$37,257,000	296

CHAPTER TWO

HOW TO GET ORGANIZED AND OPERATE THE DEPARTMENT

STANDARD OPERATING POLICIES AND PROCEDURES

Commercial loan analysis is, essentially, a control and audit function. It exists to identify various strengths and weaknesses in loan relationships. There is relatively little margin for error, and thought processes are critical as opposed to creative in nature. For this type of function, a highly structured environment is most suitable. By operating within strict guidelines, department output is uniform, accurate, and complete.

To establish a formal structure, the credit department should create a set of standard operating policies and procedures. Policies and procedures should be put into writing, and they should be distributed to department members as well as to anyone who works closely with the department.

The standard policy is also important for the credit department because credit analyst positions turn over frequently. New analysts need to become familiar with department policy and procedures fairly quickly, and this cannot occur if policy and procedures are not expressed in writing.

Credit department policy and procedures include aspects such as:

- Types of analysis performed

- Log in of analysis requests

- Determination of priorities

- Target turnaround times and distribution

- Bank-specific techniques for spreading financial statements

- Information necessary from the loan officer prior to beginning a project

- Department meetings

- Training

- Standard formats for reporting analysis

- Information storage and filing

Types of Analysis Performed

Credit department members as well as outsiders should be aware of the types of analysis available. The most basic examples of analysis include **financial statement spreadsheets** or **spreads accompanied by questions and comments**. Such questions and comments are meant to incite thoughts in the mind of the loan officer regarding structuring, and they also serve to answer analyst questions necessary to complete more detailed forms of analysis. The department should also offer individual **debt service coverage analysis** and **collateral analysis**. This type of analysis is frequently used as a feasibility measure prior to the request for completion of a full loan write-up.

The most complex form of analysis is a **full loan presentation** or a **"write-up."** The loan presentation is the report that the loan officer or the committee uses to make a decision on a new loan request. In addition, banks generally require loan renewals and annual reviews to be presented with full loan write-ups as if they are extensions of new credit.

To represent the amount of work involved in each of these projects, the following chart indicates typical completion times for each type of analysis. These are only general guidelines; actual times may vary due to experience levels of analysts and complexities of analysis.

Type of Analysis	Average Completion Time
Financial Statement Spreads	15 minutes to 2 hours
Questions and Comments on Spreads	15 minutes to 1 hour
Debt Service Coverage Analysis	15 minutes to 1 hour
Collateral Analysis	15 minutes to 1 hour
Loan Presentation	4 hours to 16 hours

Department policy should include minimum, total relationship dollar amounts over which loan analysis must be produced by the credit department. A typical policy requires relationships over a certain dollar amount to receive credit department spreads and/or debt service coverage analyses prior to approval, and relationships over an additional dollar amount to receive full loan presentations.

This policy ensures that all loan requests and loan reviews for the bank's larger relationships receive objective analysis from the credit department. In addition, the adoption of such a policy allows the analysis of extremely small relationships to remain in the hands of the lenders and their assistants, where it is performed more quickly and efficiently than in the credit department.

Department procedures should also describe when, if ever, credit analysts are expected to offer their recommendations. For example, many banks require analysts to recommend whether to approve a loan request or to recommend an appropriate risk rating or documentation necessary for a loan. If analysts are expected to provide recommendations, then supporting information for their recommendation decisions should be included in the procedures. For example, if credit analysts recommend risk ratings, then a table of risk-ratings should be provided which lists each rating and describes its characteristics.

Log-In of Analysis Requests

Whenever work is requested by a loan officer to be completed by the credit department, it should be logged in for prioritization and tracking. A central log-in form or computer spreadsheet should be created for the department. The form should include:

■ Name of applicant or borrower to be analyzed

■ Name of loan officer requesting analysis

■ Type of analysis requested

■ Deadline by which analysis is needed

■ Dollar amount of loan relationship or request and type of loan request

■ Name of assigned analyst

■ Date logged in

■ Date begun

■ Date completed

■ Estimate of total hours utilized to complete analysis

The deadline, type of analysis, size of relationship, and date logged in are used to prioritize multiple work requests. Priorities are generally determined as follows:

■ The earlier the deadline, the higher the priority.

■ The earlier the request is logged in, the higher the priority.

■ Requests for full loan presentations have priority over requests for spreads or other analyses.

■ Requests for analysis of new loans have priority over analysis of renewals, which, in turn, have priority over annual reviews.

■ The higher the dollar amount of the loan request or the loan relationship, the higher the priority.

Your bank determines which of the above determinations of priorities are most important.

Use of the log-in form also allows tracking of time spent to complete each analysis project. The department manager can track how frequently deadlines are met, turnover of work requests in days, and total time spent on each project in hours. These figures determine whether each analyst's output is timely as well as whether certain department goals, such as a five-day turnaround time, are met. A sample log-in form (Figure 2–1) appears at the end of this chapter.

Finally, use of the log-in form allows work to be assigned to the appropriate individual analyst. For example, a complex relationship should be analyzed by an experienced credit analyst, while a simpler relationship or a simpler type of analysis such as a spread can be analyzed by a newer department member.

Also, to save time, a request for a simple update of a loan analysis should be performed by the analyst who originally completed the work. However, when a year's time passes, and a loan is in need of an annual review or renewal (or whenever a loan analysis becomes dated), a different analyst should perform the work. This policy helps to ensure objectivity, and a fresh set of eyes may bring additional insight to the relationship. To further ensure objectivity, department policy should state that no department member is allowed to analyze a relationship in which he or she has a personal interest or significant personal knowledge.

Determination of Priorities

Priorities should be defined in department policy in a similar manner to those presented above. In addition, policy should detail who has the authority to approve individual exceptions to the policy on a case-by-case basis. It is important that this aspect of policy be understood by department members and outsiders. This leads to less misunderstanding regarding which projects are begun at which time.

Target Turnaround Times and Distribution

Policy should detail target turnaround times. For example, the goal of a typical credit department is to complete a loan analysis project within one week of its request by the loan officer.

Department policy may also specify that the loan presentation is not distributed to the loan officer servicing the relationship until the presentation is in its completed form. The use of this policy decreases the loan officer's ability to influence the analysis; however, it also decreases his or her ability to suggest correction of errors or omissions by the analyst. If a loan presentation is shown to anyone outside the credit department prior to its completion, it should be clearly marked as a "draft" copy to avoid confusion or misuse.

Department policy should also detail a time at which the completed loan presentation must be presented to committee members prior to a meeting. For example, a bank may require loan presentations to be distributed by a certain time in the afternoon **preceding** the day of the loan committee meeting.

Bank-Specific Analysis Techniques

The bank's preferred techniques for financial statement spreading and analysis should be detailed in credit department procedures. For example, many banks consider officer, employee, and stockholder loans as well as prepaid expenses to be **noncurrent** assets, regardless of their classification on financial statements provided by the borrower. In addition, many banks consider income tax loss carryforward and leasehold improvements to be **intangible assets**. All such special situations should be detailed in department procedures so that they are clear to the analysts and to the lenders.

Techniques for calculating and presenting debt service coverage should be included in department procedures so that analysis remains uniform. Nearly every bank and every individual presents cash flow in a slightly different manner. A uniform procedure minimizes discrepancies between cash flow analyses. Also, techniques for reporting collateral coverage, loan to values, and discounting of collateral should be included in the procedures. This also leads to uniformity of analysis and full understanding by those who use the analysis.

Obtaining Full Information

Loan analysts frequently spend great amounts of time tracking down loan officers and searching through files to find information necessary to complete loan analysis projects. A great deal of this information can be provided quickly and easily by the loan officer. Therefore, a great deal of time can be saved if the loan officer provides complete information at the time he or she requests the work.

In theory, the analyst should be provided with all necessary information to complete the analysis in full before he or she begins work on the project. Loan analysts should work on one project at a time, and finish each project in full before beginning the next. Although this cannot occur in practice, it is important to remain as close as possible to working on only one project at a time. Devoting all of one's efforts to the completion of an individual project is more efficient than moving back and forth from project to project.

An excellent way to obtain the information necessary to complete a project is to require loan officers to fill out a brief form whenever they request work from the credit department. Many banks actually require the loan officer to complete a detailed memo when requesting a loan write-up. This requirement is, however, difficult to enforce because loan officers simply do not have time to complete a full memo. On the other hand, strict requirement of a brief, hand-written form is far easier to enforce.

The form should include any background information necessary, a brief description of the business plan, and a detailed list of the terms of each loan request. A sample loan officer work-request form (Figure 2–2) appears at the end of this chapter.

Department Meetings

The frequency that the credit department meets as a group should be detailed in policy. Also, a procedure for review of each loan presentation by the department supervisor and by the other department members should be included in policy.

Information Storage and Filing

Policy and procedures regarding information storage and filing should be detailed for use of credit department and commercial lending department members. A system should be established for credit files so that each file is organized in the same manner. This allows analysts and lenders to easily find documents stored in the credit files. In addition, documents stored on computers or on a computer network should be filed according to an organized system so that they may be easily accessed for later use.

All credit files and/or collateral files containing original notes, loan agreements, mortgages, negotiable collateral, or other important original documentation should be stored in a fireproof area. Further, while a department member has a file checked out for reference or for analysis, it is his or her responsibility to ensure that the file is stored properly. At the end of each day and during periods of absence from the area, the department member should temporarily store files being used in a fireproof cabinet located in the department or in the department member's office.

Bank Loan Policy

Analysts should not only be familiar with department policy, they should also be familiar with overall bank loan policy. Familiarity with loan policy is essential because it is loan policy against which analysts compare aspects such as loan structure, pricing, and collateral for compliance. If possible, the credit department policy should actually be a component of overall bank loan policy. This ensures the importance of credit department policy, and it promotes knowledge of the policy throughout the lending area.

STANDARD LOAN PRESENTATION FORMAT

The loan presentation format is a crucial element of credit department policy. A standard format is important because the loan presentation is the primary output of the department. Familiarity with this document is important for those who will use it. More importantly, since commercial loan decisions are based on loan presentations, each must be accurate and complete. Strict use of a standard format ensures inclusion of all important aspects of loan analysis.

The loan presentation format should also be flexible enough to adapt to special situations, and it should be concise, so that it can be read in a relatively short period of time. If an aspect of the standard loan presentation does not apply or is not important to a given loan, then that aspect should be omitted.

The standard format should exist, not only in department policy, but as a template for use with the department's word processing software. The template is used as a starting point for loan presentations and is filled in appropriately. The use of such a template is an immense time-saver. A sample loan presentation form (Figure 2–3) appears at the end of this chapter.

The following list represents the major areas that the loan presentation should include as well as the details that should be addressed in each area:

Loan Presentation Information

■ Credit analyst name

■ Loan officer name

■ Date

■ Name of committee or individual who will approve, deny, or review the loan

Applicant Information

■ Name

■ Address

■ Names of managers and their titles

■ Names of owners and their percentages

■ Form of ownership (C Corporation, S Corporation, proprietorship, partnership)

■ Year business was formed

■ SIC code and its description

Credit Request

- Type of request (renewal, approval of new funds, etc.)

- Type of loan (line of credit, installment, mortgage, etc.)

- Amount of loan

- Purpose of loan/use of loan funds

- Interest rate

- Fees

- Term

- Amortization

- Collateral

- Guarantees

- Life insurance requirements

- Advance formula

- Other controls (hazard insurance, ratio, salary, bonus, dividend requirements)

- Conditions of approval

- Financial statements required periodically

Relationship Information

- Current and proposed loan relationship risk ratings

- Loan policy exceptions

- Total relationship loan commitment

- Current bank legal lending limit

- Summary of existing loan relationship (include for each loan: origination date, original commitment, current balance, current commitment, maturity date, interest rate, monthly payment, collateral, purpose).

- Summary of existing deposit relationship (include type and current balance of each deposit account plus cost of funds).

Background Information

- Background of applicant/loan relationship

- Management

- Management succession plans

- Business plans

Primary Source of Repayment Analysis

- Accrual-based cash flow analysis (include cash available calculation, debt service coverage ratio, and dollar amount of excess/deficit debt service coverage).

- Cash-basis cash flow analysis (include cash available calculation, debt service coverage ratio, and dollar amount of excess/deficit debt service coverage).

■ Debt service calculations

■ Analysis of differences between accrual- and cash-basis cash flows

■ Breakeven analysis

Secondary Source of Repayment Analysis

■ Collateral detailed by loan

■ Collateral values

■ Source of collateral values (appraisal, inventory, aging, estimate, etc.)

■ Loan to value ratios

■ Aging of accounts receivable

■ Equipment/inventory lists

Other Repayment Analysis

■ Guarantors

■ Guarantors' adjusted net worth

■ Guarantors' liquid assets

■ Date of personal financial statements used for guarantor analysis

■ Annual personal income or cash flow

■ Personal cash flow analysis

■ Credit reports (individual or business)

Financial Analysis

- Types of business financial statements analyzed (audited, compiled, reviewed, tax returns, etc.)

- Name of preparer of financial statements

- Income statement analysis (revenues, profits, margins, expenses, etc.)

- Balance sheet analysis (leverage, liquidity, turnover, line usage, etc.)

- Pro forma balance sheet after new funds are disbursed

- Projections

Business Analysis

- Industry assessment

- Customers

- Competitors

- Business risks

- Economic analysis

- Environmental considerations (explanation of risks, documentation required)

Summary of Most Important Factors

Attachments

- Financial statement spreads
- Personal financial statements
- Loan officer comments
- Charts/other information

Using Computer Technology to Get Organized and Improve Efficiency

Computer technology has had a major impact on the business world by extending its abilities and improving its efficiency. The world of banking and the commercial lending area specifically have benefited immensely from such technology.

Spreadsheet Programs

One benefit of technology is the ability to perform computerized financial statement spreading. Various software packages are available for statement spreading:

FINANCIAL STATEMENT SPREADING SOFTWARE	ADDRESS/PHONE
TurboFAST	Financial Proformas, Inc. 1855 Olympic Boulevard, Suite 200 Walnut Creek, CA 94596 (800) 321-3278
FAMAS	Crowe, Chizek and Company One American Square, Suite 3000 P.O. Box 82011 Indianapolis, IN 46282 (800) 523-2799
Ratio Master	Intex Solutions, Inc. 161 Highland Avenue Needham, MA 02194 (617) 449-6222
STAN	Baker Hill Corporation 655 West Carmel Drive, Suite 100 Carmel, IN 46032 (800) 821-2220
fisCAL	The Halycon Group One Halycon Place P.O. Box 1249 Folly Beach, SC 29439 (800) 248-5550

Balance sheet and income statement values from statements provided by the commercial borrower are input by the analyst. The program then produces detailed financial statements for multiple years presented side by side. The output includes percentages of total assets or total sales, various financial ratios, reconciliations, and cash flow statements. (Figure 2–4, a sample spreadsheet program output from TurboFAST, version 4.3, is presented at the end of this chapter.) These programs even contain modules which prepare projections or provide written analysis and questions arising from the statements.

In addition to TurboFAST, FAMAS, Ratio Master, STAN, and fisCAL, spreadsheet programs such as Lotus 1-2-3 are useful for the preparation of financial statement spreads or reports that are tailored to individual specifications.

Before spreadsheet technology existed, all spreading was performed manually. Each value was entered by hand, and each calculation was performed individually by the analyst. This process had numerous drawbacks. The repetitive calculations were prone to human error; the calculations were not standardized; and analysis and lending professionals spent a great deal of time inputting data and performing calculations (Meece 1993, 85).[1] Spreadsheet technology has drastically improved the efficiency of the credit department.

---

1 This copyrighted material is reprinted with permission from *Commercial Lending Review*, 488 Madison Avenue, New York, NY 10022.

Word Processing Programs

Word processing software also increases credit department efficiency. Word processing software such as WordPerfect can be used to prepare loan presentations and other written analysis as well as any correspondence. One advantage of the use of word processing software is that a standard loan presentation and cash flow analysis templates can be created to serve as starting points for loan analysis. The use of such templates leads to uniformity of analysis among department members.

Another advantage of using word processing software is that each document can be stored and organized for future reference. Each commercial customer should have its own subdirectory (or electronic file created to contain customer documents) in DOS. Each piece of analysis and all correspondence for a given customer should be stored in this subdirectory. If the bank has a computer network, then the customer subdirectories should be accessible to all commercial lending and credit analysis personnel. These subdirectories serve as convenient electronic files, which can replace physical credit files and paperwork.

Such information should be "backed up" (that is, copied to separate disks or tapes) frequently, and the back-up disks or tapes should be stored at a different location than the main computer or file server. This ensures that in case of an accident or disaster, the information will not be lost. This is especially important for computer information that is not stored elsewhere in hard copy form.

Such information should also be kept confidential. Only the commercial lending and credit areas should have access to these computer files. Passwords or some other type of access control should exist to ensure that the records are accessible only by the appropriate personnel.

Summary

Credit Department organization is extremely important. Organization tasks include prioritization and tracking of work; implementation of procedures to obtain full information necessary for analysis projects; standardization of policies, procedures, and reporting; and use of technology to become more efficient. Organization allows department members to better understand what is expected, what is important, how to analyze, and how to report, and it also provides analysts with the tools necessary to be effective and efficient. The result is more accurate and complete loan analysis produced in a more efficient manner.

Sources

First of America Bank Corporation. *Instructions for Preparation of Commercial Loan Applications under the June 1991 Revised FOABC Standardized Format*. June 1991.

Hoffman, Margaret A., and Fischer, Gerald C. *Credit Department Management*. (Philadelphia: Robert Morris Associates, 1980), 86–92.

Meece, David C. "A Low-Cost Statement Spreader for Small Banks." *Commercial Lending Review*. Vol. 8, No. 3 (Summer 1993), 85–89.

FIGURE 2–1: CREDIT DEPARTMENT WORK REQUEST LOG-IN FORM

NAME OF BORROWER OR APPLICANT	LOAN OFFICER	TYPE OF ANALYSIS	LOAN	DEAD-LINE	DATE REC.	DATE BEGUN	DATE COMP.	HOURS SPENT	ANALYST

FIGURE 2–2: LOAN OFFICER REQUEST FORM FOR LOAN ANALYSIS

Today's Date:	Requested Completion Date:
Applicant/Borrower Name:	Loan Officer:
Background:	Business Plan:

Loan Request 1:
Purpose:
Pricing:
Repayment Terms:
Collateral:
Additional Support/Guarantees:
Controls/Advance Formula:

Loan Request 2:
Purpose:
Pricing:
Repayment Terms:
Collateral:
Additional Support/Guarantees:
Controls/Advance Formula:

Loan Request 3:
Purpose:
Pricing:
Repayment Terms:
Collateral:
Additional Support/Guarantees:
Controls/Advance Formula:

FIGURE 2–3: SAMPLE LOAN PRESENTATION FORM

MEMORANDUM

Date:

To: *Approving body*
From: *Analyst name, title*
         Servicing officer name, title
Re: *Loan request for name of applicant*

APPLICANT INFORMATION:

APPLICANT	OWNER/ OFFICER	% OF OWNERSHIP	TITLE	YEARS EXPERIENCE
applicant name	*officer #1 name*	*ownership %*	*title*	*experience*
address	*officer #2 name*	*ownership %*	*title*	*experience*
address	*officer #3 name*	*ownership %*	*title*	*experience*
address	*officer #4 name*	*ownership %*	*title*	*experience*

Form of Ownership of Applicant: _____ / Date Business Was Formed: _____
SIC Code: _____ / Description of SIC Code: _____

LOAN REQUEST INFORMATION:

Loan Request:	*for example, "Approval of $100,000 Line of Credit"*
Purpose:	*purpose for loan/use of loan funds*
Pricing:	*interest rate, fees, prepayment penalty*
Repayment Terms:	*term and amortization periods*
Collateral:	*collateral*
Additional Support:	*guarantees, life insurance requirements*
Controls:	*advance formula, borrowing base, disbursement, or other controls*
Conditions of Approval:	*financial statement requirements/other conditions*

FIGURE 2–3 (continued)

RELATIONSHIP INFORMATION:
Current Relationship Risk Rating:___ / Proposed Relationship Risk Rating:__
Rationale for Proposed Risk Rating:

_____

_____

_____

_____

Proposed Total Bank Commitment: ___
Proposed Total Holding Company Commitment: ___
Current Bank Legal Lending Limit: ___
Proposed Exceptions to Bank Loan Policy:

_____

_____

_____

_____

CURRENT LENDING RELATIONSHIP:

ORIG. DATE	ORIG. COMMIT.	CURRENT BALANCE	CURRENT COMMIT.	MATURE DATE	INT. RATE	MONTHLY PAYMENT	COLL-ATERAL	PURPOSE
date	commit.	balance	commit.	date	rate	payment	coll.	purpose
date	commit.	balance	commit.	date	rate	payment	coll.	purpose
date	commit.	balance	commit.	date	rate	payment	coll.	purpose
date	commit.	balance	commit.	date	rate	payment	coll.	purpose

CURRENT DEPOSIT RELATIONSHIP:

TYPE OF DEPOSIT	CURRENT BALANCE	AVERAGE BALANCE	INTEREST RATE
type	balance	avg. balance	rate
type	balance	avg. balance	rate
TOTAL:	total balance	total avg. balance	N/A

FIGURE 2–3 (continued)

BACKGROUND INFORMATION:
Applicant/Loan Relationship:

_____
_____
_____
_____
_____

Management:

_____
_____
_____
_____

Management Succession Plans:

_____
_____
_____
_____
_____

Business Plans:

_____
_____
_____
_____
_____

FIGURE 2–3 (Continued)

PRIMARY SOURCE OF REPAYMENT ANALYSIS:

ACCRUAL-BASIS CASH FLOW	INTERIM PERIOD ENDED: ___	FISCAL YEAR ENDED: ___	FISCAL YEAR ENDED: ___	FISCAL YEAR ENDED: ___
Net Income	$	$	$	$
Add: Deprec.	$	$	$	$
Add: Interest	$	$	$	$
TOTAL AVAILABLE	$	$	$	$
Coverage Ratio	%	%	%	%
Excess/Deficit	$	$	$	$

CASH-BASIS CASH FLOW	INTERIM PERIOD ENDED: ___	FISCAL YEAR ENDED: ___	FISCAL YEAR ENDED: ___	FISCAL YEAR ENDED: ___
Net Cash After Operations	$	$	$	$
Coverage Ratio	%	%	%	%
Excess/Deficit	$	$	$	$

PROPOSED DEBT SERVICE REQUIREMENTS:

LOAN	AMOUNT	AMORTIZATION	INTEREST RATE	MONTHLY PAYMENT	ANNUAL PAYMENT
loan	$	amortization	%	$	$
loan	$	amortization	%	$	$
loan	$	amortization	%	$	$
loan	$	amortization	%	$	$

Total Annual Debt Service Requirement: $_____

Analysis of Cash Flow:

_____

_____

_____

Breakeven Analysis:

_____

_____

_____

FIGURE 2–3 (Continued)

SECONDARY SOURCE OF REPAYMENT ANALYSIS:

LOAN/AMOUNT	COLLATERAL	VALUE	SOURCE	LOAN TO VALUE
$	collateral	$	source	%
$	collateral	$	source	%
$	collateral	$	source	%
$	collateral	$	source	%

Aggregate Loan to Value: $_____
Aggregate Loan to Discounted Value: $_____

SCHEDULE OF DISCOUNTED ASSETS:

ASSET	BOOK VALUE	ADVANCE RATE	DISCOUNTED VALUE
asset	$	%	$
asset	$	%	$
asset	$	%	$
TOTAL	$	N/A	$

ACCOUNTS RECEIVABLE AGING	AMOUNT	PERCENTAGE
Current	$	%
31-60 days past due	$	%
61-90 days past due	$	%
over 90 days past due	$	%
TOTAL	$	100%

Equipment/Inventory Listing:

_____

_____

_____

Collateral Analysis:

_____

_____

_____

Figure 2–3 (Continued)

Other Repayment Analysis:

Guarantors	Adjusted Net Worth	Liquid Assets	Personal Financial Statement Date
name	$	$	date
name	$	$	date
TOTAL	$	$	N/A

Annual Personal Income/Personal Cash Flow Analysis:

_____

_____

Credit Report Results:

_____

_____

Financial Analysis:

Types of Financial Statements Analyzed/Preparer/Reliability:

_____

_____

Historical Income Statement Analysis:

_____

_____

Historical Balance Sheet Analysis:

_____

_____

Projections/Pro Forma Analysis:

_____

_____

FIGURE 2–3 (Continued)

BUSINESS ANALYSIS:
Industry Analysis/Business Risk Analysis:

_____

_____

_____

Customer/Competitor Analysis:

_____

_____

_____

Local/National/International Economic Analysis:

_____

_____

_____

Environmental Analysis/Documentation:

_____

_____

_____

SUMMARY OF MOST IMPORTANT FACTORS:

_____

_____

_____

LIST OF ATTACHMENTS:

_____

_____

_____

_____

Figure 2–4: Sample Spreadsheet Program Output ✗

CHARLIE'S CHOCOLATE COMPANY, INC.

| FAST 4.3 | Common Size Report | | | | | 03/24/94 | |
| General Industries | | | | | | 09:28 A.M. | |

SIC Code : 2064_

		COMPILE		COMPILE		COMPILE	
Auditor : Ryan Jones, CPA		Dec 31		Dec 31		Dec 31	
Analyst : Ken Pirok		1993		1992		1991	
AMOUNTS IN THOUSANDS OF DOLLARS		12 Mth		12 Mth		12 Mth	
COMMON SIZE REPORT		$	%	$	%	$	%
ASSETS:							
Cash		0	0.0	28	5.0	44	8.1
Accounts Receivable - Trade		277	35.9	151	26.8	95	17.6
Raw Materials		266	34.5	172	30.5	135	25.0
Finished Goods		32	4.1	25	4.4	30	5.6
Total Inventory		298	38.6	197	34.9	165	30.6
TOTAL CURRENT ASSETS		575	74.5	376	66.7	304	56.3
Machinery & Equipment		280	36.3	228	40.4	228	42.2
Transportation Equipment		15	1.9	15	2.7	15	2.8
Gross Fixed Assets		295	38.2	243	43.1	243	45.0
Less: Accumulated Depreciation		164	21.2	109	19.3	59	10.9
Total Fixed Assets - Net		131	17.0	134	23.8	184	34.1
Due from Employees		12	1.6	0	0.0	0	0.0
Prepaid Expenses - Noncurrent		39	5.1	34	6.0	27	5.0
INTANGIBLES							
Goodwill - Net		15	1.9	20	3.5	25	4.6
NONCURRENT ASSETS		197	25.5	188	33.3	236	43.7
TOTAL ASSETS		772	100.0	564	100.0	540	100.0

FIGURE 2–4 (Continued)

CHARLIE'S CHOCOLATE COMPANY, INC.

FAST 4.3	Common Size Report				03/24/94	
General Industries					09:28 A.M.	

SIC Code : 2064_

Auditor : Ryan Jones, CPA	COMPILE		COMPILE		COMPILE	
Analyst : Ken Pirok	Dec 31		Dec 31		Dec 31	
	1993		1992		1991	
AMOUNTS IN THOUSANDS OF DOLLARS	12 Mth		12 Mth		12 Mth	
LIABILITIES	$	%	$	%	$	%
Overdraft	41	5.3	0	0.0	0	0.0
Notes Payable S/T - Bank	100	13.0	36	6.4	5	0.9
Current Maturities LTD - 1	40	5.2	30	5.3	30	5.6
Accounts Payable - Trade	103	13.3	45	8.0	50	9.3
Wages/Salaries Payable	19	2.5	15	2.7	5	0.9
Interest Payable	3	0.4	0	0.0	0	0.0
Total Accrued Liabilities	22	2.8	15	2.7	5	0.9
TOTAL CURRENT LIABILITIES	306	39.6	126	22.3	90	16.7
Exist Long Term Debt - 1	288	37.3	260	46.1	290	53.7
TOTAL SENIOR LT LIABILITIES	288	37.3	260	46.1	290	53.7
TOTAL SENIOR LIABILITIES	594	76.9	386	68.4	380	70.4
Subordinated Debt - 1	75	9.7	75	13.3	75	13.9
TOTAL LIABILITIES	669	86.7	461	81.7	455	84.3
NET WORTH						
Common Stock	1	0.1	1	0.2	1	0.2
Paid In Capital	99	12.8	99	17.6	99	18.3
Retained Earnings	3	0.4	3	0.5	-15	-2.8
NET WORTH	103	13.3	103	18.3	85	15.7
TOTAL LIABILITIES & NET WORTH	772	100.0	564	100.0	540	100.0
Tangible Net Worth	88	11.4	83	14.7	60	11.1
Working Capital	269	34.8	250	44.3	214	39.6

FIGURE 2–4 (Continued)

CHARLIE'S CHOCOLATE COMPANY, INC.

| FAST 4.3 | Common Size Report | | | | | | 03/24/94 |
| General Industries | | | | | | | 09:28 A.M. |

SIC Code : 2064_							
Auditor : Ryan Jones, CPA	COMPILE		COMPILE		COMPILE		
Analyst : Ken Pirok	Dec 31		Dec 31		Dec 31		
	1993		1992		1991		
AMOUNTS IN THOUSANDS OF DOLLARS	12 Mth		12 Mth		12 Mth		
INCOME STATEMENT	$	%	$	%	$	%	
Sales (Product 1)	1,290	100.0	957	100.0	795	100.0	
Cost of Goods Sold (Product 1)	654	50.7	458	47.9	400	50.3	
Depreciation in CoGS	30	2.3	25	2.6	25	3.1	
GROSS PROFIT/REVENUES	606	47.0	474	49.5	370	46.5	
General & Administrative Expense	301	23.3	244	25.5	230	28.9	
Officers Compensation	105	8.1	50	5.2	30	3.8	
Lease & Rental Expense	110	8.5	100	10.4	100	12.6	
Bad Debt Expense	16	1.2	0	0.0	0	0.0	
Depreciation	25	1.9	25	2.6	10	1.3	
Amortization	5	0.4	5	0.5	5	0.6	
TOTAL OPERATING EXPENSES	562	43.6	424	44.3	375	47.2	
OPERATING INCOME	44	3.4	50	5.2	-5	-0.6	
Interest Expense ST	36	2.8	27	2.8	21	2.6	
TOTAL INTEREST EXPENSE	36	2.8	27	2.8	21	2.6	
Gain on Sale of Assets	12	0.9	0	0.0	0	0.0	
Charitable Contributions	10	0.8	0	0.0	0	0.0	
NET PROFIT	10	0.8	23	2.4	-26	-3.3	
Cash Dividend - Common Stock	10	0.8	5	0.5	0	0.0	
CHANGE IN NET WORTH	0	0.0	18	1.9	-26	-3.3	

FIGURE 2–4 (Continued)

CHARLIE'S CHOCOLATE COMPANY, INC.		
FAST 4.3 · · · · · Cash Flow		03/24/94
General Industries		09:28 A.M.
SIC Code : 2064_		
Auditor : Ryan Jones, CPA	COMPILE	COMPILE
Analyst : Ken Pirok	Dec 31	Dec 31
	1993	1992
AMOUNTS IN THOUSANDS OF DOLLARS	12 Mth	12 Mth
CASHFLOW		
Sales - Net	1,290	957
Change in Receivables	-126	-56
CASH FROM SALES	1,164	901
Cost of Goods Sold	-654	-458
Change in Inventories	-101	-32
Change in Payables	58	-5
CASH PRODUCTION COSTS	-697	-495
GROSS CASH PROFITS	467	406
SG & A Expense	-532	-394
Change in Prepaids	-5	-7
Change in Accruals	4	10
Cash Operating Expense	-533	-391
CASH AFTER OPERATIONS	-66	15
Miscellaneous Cash Income	-22	0
NET CASH AFTER OPERATIONS	-88	15
Interest Expense	-33	-27
Dividends Paid	-10	-5
Financing Costs	-43	-32
NET CASH INCOME	-131	-17
Current Portion Long-Term Debt	-30	-30
CASH AFTER DEBT AMORTIZATION	-161	-47
Capital Expenditures - Tangible	-40	0
FINANCING SURPLUS (REQUIREMENTS)	-201	-47
Change in Short-Term Debt	105	31
Change in Long-Term Debt	68	0
Total External Financing	173	31
Cash After Financing	-28	-16
Actual Change in Cash	-28	-16
Net Income + Depreciation	70	78
Misc Cash Income Detail:		
Other Noncurrent Assets	-12	0
Other Expense	-10	0
Total	-22	0

FIGURE 2–4 (Continued)

CHARLIE'S CHOCOLATE COMPANY, INC.

FAST 4.3	Financial Ratios		03/24/94
General Industries			09:28 A.M.

SIC Code : 2064_			
Auditor : Ryan Jones, CPA	COMPILE	COMPILE	COMPILE
Analyst : Ken Pirok	Dec 31	Dec 31	Dec 31
	1993	1992	1991
AMOUNTS IN THOUSANDS OF DOLLARS	12 Mth	12 Mth	12 Mth

√ FINANCIAL RATIOS

GROWTH RATIOS:			
Net Sales Growth, Composite %	34.80	20.38	N/A
Sales Growth, Sales (Product 1)	34.80	20.38	N/A
Net Income Growth, %	-56.52	188.46	N/A
Total Assets Growth, %	36.88	4.44	N/A
Total Liabilities Growth, %	45.12	1.32	N/A
Net Worth Growth, %	0.00	21.18	N/A
√ **PROFITABILITY RATIOS:**			
Gross Margin, Composite %	49.30	52.14	49.69
Margin, Sales (Product 1)	49.30	52.14	49.69
SG & A, %	41.24	41.17	45.28
Cushion (Gross Margin - SG & A), %	8.06	10.97	4.40
Depreciation, Amortization, %	4.65	5.75	5.03
Operating Profit Margin, %	3.41	5.22	-0.63
Interest Expense, %	2.79	2.82	2.64
Operating Margin, %	0.62	2.40	-3.27
Net Margin, %	0.78	2.40	-3.27
Return on Average Assets, %	1.50	4.17	N/A
Return on Average Equity, %	11.70	32.17	N/A
Dividend Payout Rate, %	100.00	21.74	0.00
COVERAGE RATIOS:			
EBITDA/(Total Interest + CMLTD)	N/A	1.84	N/A
Interest Coverage (EBIT/Interest)	1.28	1.85	-0.24
Net Income + Depreciation/CMLTD	2.33	2.60	N/A
ACTIVITY RATIOS:			
Receivables in Days	78	58	44
Inventory in Days	166	157	151
Payables in Days	57	36	46
Total Assets/Net sales	0.60	0.59	0.68

FIGURE 2–4 (Continued)

LIQUIDITY RATIOS:			
Working Capital	269	250	214
Quick Ratio	0.91	1.42	1.54
Current Ratio	1.88	2.98	3.38
Sales/Net Working Capital	4.80	3.83	3.71
LEVERAGE RATIOS:			
Total Liabilities/Total Net Worth	7.60	5.55	7.58
Tot Sr. Liabs./TNW & Sub Debt	3.64	2.44	2.81
Borrowed Funds/TNW & Sub Debt	2.88	2.06	2.41
Long-Term Debt/Net Fixed Assets	2.50	2.16	1.74
CASH POSITION:			
Cash Margin %	36.20	42.42	N/A
Cash Coverage	-1.21	0.24	N/A
Net Cash Income	N/A	-17	N/A
Net Income + Depreciation	70	78	14
SUSTAINABLE GROWTH & BANKRUPTCY:			
Sustainable Growth, (N/(T-N)) %	0.00	12.34	N/A
$Z=1.2x1 +1.4x2 +3.3x3 +.6x4 +.999x5$	2.38	2.66	1.99

CHAPTER THREE

COMMUNICATION AND RESEARCH

COMMUNICATION

Communication is an important aspect of effective credit department management. It is important that regular and open communication occurs between the supervisor and each individual department member as well as among department members and between the credit department and the other areas of the bank.

DEPARTMENT MEETINGS

An excellent way to encourage communication is for the entire credit department to meet periodically as a group. A regular meeting should be held about once per week, and special meetings should occur whenever the need arises. The agenda may include discussion of pending work and work assignments, new issues or announcements, and questions and explanations concerning loan analysis. Communication through group meetings (as well as through one-on-one conversation) is especially important during bank examinations and mergers or when new members join the department.

Meetings should also be held to discuss each loan presentation before it is provided by the analyst to the loan officer or loan committee. Each department member should read the loan presentation, evaluate it, and formulate questions. A brief meeting of the department should then be held to discuss the analysis. The advantage of such group discussion is that any potential questions or problems are addressed before the final product is presented. Credit department members can point out any errors, omissions, or methods of analysis that might have been overlooked by the analyst. Further, any notable aspects of the loan analysis can be presented to the other analysts during the meeting.

COMMUNICATION WITH OFFICERS AND COMMITTEES

Another way to increase communication is to allow analysts to attend loan committee meetings. Observation of loan committee meetings increases understanding of the approval process as well as loan structuring and loan administration; loan committee observation also teaches which aspects of loan analysis are most important to the bank.

In addition, when analysts attend loan committee meetings, they are available to answer questions and to provide comments on their loan presentations. Loan committee members frequently have questions concerning financial statement spreads, debt service coverage calculations, collateral valuations, or loan policy issues, which can be answered by credit analysts. Also, the analyst can defend his or her figures, recommendations, or risk-rating proposals to the committee.

Communication between analysts and loan officers outside of the committee should also be highly encouraged. Loan officer experience should be shared with analysts as much as possible. Analysts should be encouraged to ask questions of loan officers to increase commercial lending knowledge. A good way to encourage communication is to institute a series of lunches between each analyst and each lender.

CUSTOMER CALLS

Improved analysis quality and increased commercial lending knowledge also result when analysts are allowed to attend customer calls with loan officers. Loan analysis is improved since the analyst is allowed to ask a few questions directly of the borrower, and because he or she experiences business operations in person. Commercial lending knowledge increases because the analyst directly observes negotiation and loan structuring with the borrower.

Also, attending customer calls helps analysts improve communication and selling skills. Going on calls even increases morale since customer calls are interesting, and since they represent a significant responsibility. Customer calls should, however, be limited to more experienced analysts, since meeting with the borrower can hinder an analyst's objectivity.

ASSIGN SPECIAL PROJECTS

An excellent way to improve the credit department is to assign research and reporting projects to the analysts. Single areas of interest relevant to multiple commercial loan presentations can be completed once by an analyst and updated periodically for use in all loan presentations. Further, various topics of interest to bank management can be analyzed and reported by credit analysts. Examples of credit analyst research or reporting topics include:

- Local economy

- Local real estate market

- Portfolio concentrations

- Analysis of industries that are prevalent in the bank's market area or that are prevalent in the bank's loan portfolio

- Reporting of loan ratings

- Calculation of legal lending limit and aggregate debt amounts to test against legal lending limit

- Loan committee minutes (see Chapter 7)

- Loan pricing analysis and reporting (see Chapter 7)

- Loan loss reserve sufficiency analysis (see Chapter 7)

There are various advantages to assigning such projects. Special projects keep analysts busy during slow times, and they break monotony by allowing analysts to work on something other than loan analysis.

In addition, allowing analysts to specialize in specific industries or areas of expertise has less obvious advantages. Specialization and division of labor are more efficient than having all analysts review every aspect of loan analysis for each loan presentation. Further, specialization provides something for each analyst to call his or her own; it fosters feelings of self-worth, importance, and differentiation from others.

Although specialization and division of labor have various advantages, there are drawbacks to their implementation as well. For example, loan presentation projects should not be broken into specialties performed by various individuals. This division of labor results in analysts who are familiar with only one aspect of loan analysis and, therefore, hinders their development into managers or lenders. In addition, such an effort is difficult to coordinate; it results in inefficiency and slow completion times.

SOURCES OF INFORMATION

Industry and Economic Information

Information for research projects can be obtained from various sources. The local area economic development company and the Chamber of Commerce have information on the local economy. The local board of realtors has statistics on the real estate market.

The *U.S. Industrial Outlook* contains forecasts for 350 industries. It is published annually by the U.S. Department of Commerce, International Trade Commission, and it can be ordered through the Superintendent of Documents, Department DM, Washington, DC 20402 or by calling (800) 553-6847. In addition, trade publications for specific industries can be located through *U.S. Industrial Outlook* references or by simply asking your borrowers about them. Publishers of trade journals or magazines will almost always send a free, sample copy of their publication upon request.

The Robert Morris Associates (the association of bank loan and credit officers, or the RMA) publishes various articles and books about specific industries and specific types of commercial lending. The RMA also publishes the *Annual Statement Studies*. This publication contains general guidelines of the financial structure and operations for various industries. It includes balance sheet and income statement data as well as financial ratios for typical firms in nearly 400 lines of business.

Commercial Lending Information

Analysts should also be encouraged to spend a short time each day or each week reading publications relevant to commercial lending. Robert Morris Associates' *Journal of Commercial Lending* and the American Bankers Association's *Commercial Lending Review* are excellent sources of information. Each addresses both fundamental and new loan analysis techniques as well as techniques for analysis of particular industries and types of businesses.

In addition to periodicals, Irwin Professional Publishing publishes various lending reference books such as *Commercial Loan Analysis* also by this author. The Robert Morris Associates and the American Bankers Association also publish various reference books.

The Appraisal Foundation and the Association of Machinery and Equipment Appraisers can provide various information regarding collateral analysis. Their addresses and phone numbers as well as those of Irwin Professional Publishing, the Robert Morris Associates, and the American Bankers Association are presented below:

SOURCE OF INFORMATION	ADDRESS/PHONE
Irwin Professional Publishing (*Commercial Loan Analysis*)	1333 Burr Ridge Parkway Burr Ridge, IL 60521 (800) 634-3966
Robert Morris Associates (*Journal of Commercial Lending* and *Annual Statement Studies*)	One Liberty Place 1650 Market Street, Suite 2300 Philadelphia, PA 19103-7398 (800) 677-7621
American Bankers Association (*Commercial Lending Review*)	1120 Connecticut Avenue N.W. Washington, DC 20036 (800) 338-0626
The Appraisal Foundation	1029 Vermont Avenue, N.W., Suite 900 Washington, DC 20005-3517 (202) 347-7722
Association of Machinery and Equipment Appraisers	1110 Spring Street Silver Spring, MD 20910 (301) 587-9335

Banking and Business Information

Analysts should be encouraged to read banking and business publications. Publications such as *United States Banker, Banking Journal, American Banker,* and *Banking Week* allow analysts to remain updated on developments in the banking industry. Publications such as *The Wall Street Journal, Barron's, Business Week, Forbes, Inc., Nation's Business,* and *Small Business Success* not only update analysts on the business world, but they provide valuable information for economic and industry analysis projects. A list of publications is given below:

NAME OF PUBLICATION	PUBLISHER	SUBSCRIPTIONS-ADDRESS	SUBSCRIPTIONS-PHONE
United States Banker	Faulkner & Gray, Inc.	General Banking Division Faulkner & Gray Eleven Penn Plaza New York, NY 10001	(800) 535-8403
Banking Journal	American Bankers Association	American Bankers Association 1120 Connecticut Avenue N.W. Washington, DC 20036	(800) 338-0626
American Banker	Thompson Publications	American Banker Attn: Circulation One State Street Plaza New York, NY 10004	(800) 221-1809
Banking Week	Thompson Publications	Banking Week Attn: Circulation One State Street Plaza New York, NY 10004	(800) 221-1809

NAME OF PUBLICATION	PUBLISHER	SUBSCRIPTIONS-ADDRESS	SUBSCRIPTIONS-PHONE
The Wall Street Journal	Dow Jones & Company, Inc.	The Wall Street Journal 200 Burnett Road Chicopee, MA 01020	(800) 221-1940
Barron's	Dow Jones & Company, Inc.	Barron's 200 Burnett Road Chicopee, MA 01020	(800) 277-4136
Business Week	McGraw-Hill, Inc.	Business Week McGraw-Hill Building 1221 Avenue of the Americas New York, NY 10020	(800) 635-1200
Forbes	Forbes, Inc.	Forbes P.O. Box 10048 Des Moines, IA 50340-0048	(800) 888-9896
INC.	Goldhirsh Group, Inc.	INC. Magazine P.O. Box 54129 Boulder, CO 80322-4129	(800) 234-0999
Nation's Business	United States Chamber of Commerce	Nation's Business 1615 H Street N.W. Washington, DC 20062-2000	(800) 638-6582
Small Business Success	BankLine/Irwin Professional Publishing	BankLine 1333 Burr Ridge Parkway Burr Ridge, IL 60521	(800) 634-3966

Articles relevant to commercial lending and to special analysis projects should be clipped out or copied and kept in a central file. All analysts benefit because they are able to consult the central file for articles whenever specific needs arise. Although the reading of articles should not have a higher priority than loan analysis duties, reading and re-search as time permits will provide higher-quality analyses as well as a break in the day from a busy analysis schedule.

GENERAL TECHNICAL WRITING SKILLS

The analyst should avoid the use of unnecessarily large words and unnecessarily wordy sentences. Although it is im-portant to write in a professional manner, it is more impor-tant to write clearly and concisely. This results from the use of short, familiar, objective words as well as short, descrip-tive sentences comprising well-organized paragraphs.

The analyst should highlight each issue that he or she believes to be important. In addition, a summary should be provided with written analysis that lists the major issues and conclusions clearly for the reader.

As a final step, the analyst should revise all written work. Revision is best performed a few hours after finishing the draft or the next day. This allows the analyst to look at the presentation with a fresh eye. Revision should also in-clude spell checking the document if it was produced using word processing software.

Finally, the department should have a dictionary avail-able for use during the writing process. It is also a good idea to have a grammar and usage manual and/or a business writ-ing manual available for consultation. The following list de-tails a few of the business writing, grammar, and spelling aids that would be helpful to the credit department:

TITLE	AUTHOR	PUBLISHER
Business Communication Today (Second Edition)	Courtland Bovee and John Thill	Random House, Inc.
The New Webster's Grammar Guide	Madeline Semmelmeyer and Donald O. Bolander	Berkley Publishing Group
A Pocket Guide to Correct Grammar (Second Edition)	Vincent F. Hopper, Cedric Gale, and Ronald C. Foote, Revised by Benjamin W. Griffith	Barron's Educational Series, Inc.
The Bad Speller's Dictionary	Joseph Krevisky and Jordan L. Linfield	Random House, Inc.
Misspeller's Dictionary	N/A	Prentice Hall

SPECIFIC LOAN PRESENTATION SKILLS

When preparing the loan presentation, it is important for the analyst to uncover underlying activities and trends rather than simply restating financial statement values. Quality analysis explores and uncovers the true cause.

For example, it is insufficient to state that sales increased by 25 percent. Perhaps sales volume increased, perhaps prices were raised, or perhaps both occurred. Assume that increased sales volume was the primary contributor to the increased sales. It is necessary to explore even further to uncover the cause of the increased sales volume. Perhaps a new product was successfully introduced, or perhaps the sales force was increased or improved. These details are a crucial part of financial statement analysis.

The commercial loan presentation should remain objective and avoid judgment. The analyst's job is to present the facts, upon which the loan officer or committee makes a judgment. The analyst should avoid the use of judgmental words such as "excellent" or "poor." Whenever judgments, opinions, or unsubstantiated facts are used in the loan presentation, the source should be given. For example, "According to the loan officer, management ability is perceived to be excellent."

Even if the analyst is expected to provide a recommendation, the text of the analysis should remain objective. Only the summary or the section where the recommendation is made should contain the analyst's opinion. In addition, the analyst should support his or her recommendation with facts and figures from the analysis.

There is often more than one way to present a certain situation in the loan presentation. For example, the historical cash flow of a company may be inadequate to service a proposed loan; however, with officer salaries and dividends added back to this same cash flow, the company may be able to service the debt. It is unclear, however, which cash flow method is more appropriate. In these situations it is best to present both methods. The analyst should remain objective, and the loan officer or committee should decide which method is more appropriate.

When the loan presentation is finished, a checklist can help the analyst determine whether the analysis is complete. A sample loan presentation checklist (Figure 3–1) appears at the end of this chapter.

As a final step, each loan presentation should be read by the other department members and discussed as a group before being presented in final form. The discussion should address writing issues, and it should represent the final step in revision. Any unclear areas, any incorrect spelling or grammar, and any failures to remain objective should be communicated to the analyst. Such discussion leads to a higher-quality work product and to improvement in the writing skills of each department member.

SUMMARY

Communication is the vital link between the credit department and the rest of the bank as well as the vital link between department members. Writing skills are important because it is the credit department's written work that is used to support the loan decision. Credit analysts should be encouraged to learn from each other, from the commercial lenders, and through research and reading. The result of increased communication is more knowledgeable credit analysts who produce clear, accurate loan analyses.

SOURCES

Bovee, Courtland L., and Thill, John, V. *Business Communication Today*, 2 (New York: Random House, 1986), 30–53, 121–149, 367–396.

Schatz, Edward K. "New People, Policies, and Places: How to Manage a Credit Department Merger." *The Journal of Commercial Lending*. (February 1994), 26–31.

✓ FIGURE 3–1: LOAN PRESENTATION CHECKLIST

_____   If exceptions to policy exist or are proposed, then note each exception in the policy exception area.

_____   Analyze management, its experience level, plans for succession, and life insurance requirements.

_____   Analyze the business plan. If a business plan is not provided, then note this fact in the presentation summary.

_____   Because cash flow is generally the primary source of repayment for a loan, it is important to accurately and completely present its analysis. Double-check the figures in the cash flow analysis for accuracy. Also, a description of the cash flow analysis should be included in the presentation summary. (Be sure to analyze the swing factors if cash-basis cash flow differs significantly from accrual-basis cash flow. See Chapter 4.)

_____   If a break even analysis is appropriate, present it in the primary source of repayment section.

_____   It is generally appropriate to determine collateral liquidation values along with the loan officer for presentation in the write-up. It is, however, also recommended to obtain accounts receivable agings and inventory and equipment lists for verification. If such lists are necessary for accurate collateral analysis but are not provided, then note this in the presentation summary. Also, since collateral is important as the secondary source of repayment, its analysis should be briefly discussed in the presentation summary.

Figure 3–1 (Continued)

_____ Include industry averages such as those provided by the RMA on the financial statements for comparison. Also, include comparisons in the income statement and balance sheet analyses.

_____ If the company has a line of credit, detail the usage of the line over the past year in the balance sheet analysis.

_____ If a line of credit is proposed, then controls such as an advance ratio or a cleanup period may be required. If so, be sure to include the requirements in the detail of the loan request. If controls are not required, then it may be appropriate to mention their exclusion (and the reasons for exclusion) in the presentation summary. (Also, note that inventory and accounts receivable are typically advanced upon when a formula is used; however, fixed assets are generally excluded.)

_____ If new debt is proposed, present the pro forma debt to worth including the new debt in the balance sheet analysis. If debt is becoming subordinated as a result of the transaction, then present the senior debt to tangible net worth ratio after subordination.

_____ If the business provides projections, be sure to analyze them. If projections are not supplied, or if they are not supported by assumptions or plans, then make note of this in the presentation summary. If the business provided projections in the past, then compare them to the actual figures that occurred.

_____ The overall analysis should attempt to explore "why" certain events and figures occur in addition to stating the numbers.

Figure 3–1 (Continued)

_____   The analysis should remain completely objective.

_____   When the presentation is completed, spell check it using the word processing software.

CHAPTER FOUR

TRAINING

FORMAL TRAINING

Informal (on-the-job) training is extremely important and is often used to train commercial loan analysts. Most new analysts are trained by performing actual loan analysis and by learning from their mistakes. On-the-job training is essential because it provides actual experience that cannot be achieved in any other manner; however, the exclusive use of this method is flawed since the new analyst does not benefit from the experience of his or her coworkers, and because he or she inevitably makes many of the same mistakes that the experienced analysts once made.

Therefore, some level of formal, structured training is necessary to complement informal training. This is especially true for new analysts, but it also applies to experienced analysts who require continuing education. Formal training consists of both verbal and written instruction.

Verbal instruction should include one-on-one conversation with new analysts before, during, and after their first analysis projects. Verbal instruction should also include periodic group instruction for the entire department.

In addition, it is extremely helpful to have written tools such as training manuals and reference guides for the department. Such books can be quite inexpensive. The author has written a training manual entitled *Commercial Loan Analysis*, and the Robert Morris Associates offer various titles for analysis training (see Chapter 3 for more information).

Your department can also generate training materials itself. The benefits of an internally prepared training manual include cost savings, specific instructions tailored to your bank, and the fact that creation of a training manual is an excellent project for an experienced analyst.

SAMPLE TRAINING SCHEDULE FOR NEW ANALYSTS

Week One

- Read loan analysis instruction materials and articles.

- Read department policy and standard loan analysis formats.

- Read bank loan policy.

- Become familiar with credit files and their organization.

- Spread a basic income statement and balance sheet with direct instruction from an experienced analyst.

Week Two

- Learn basic loan structuring (pricing, types of loan facilities, term and amortization, collateral and collateral analysis, and guarantees).

- Become familiar with the concept of accrual versus cash accounting.

- Become familiar with the statement of cash flows.

- Spread more challenging financial statements.

- Perform basic analysis of ratios and cash flow.

Week Three

- Learn about risk rating and other details of loan policy.

- Learn complexities of the statement of cash flows and cash flow analysis.

- Complete a basic full loan analysis and presentation.

Week Four

- Learn more complicated loan structuring (advance formulas, controls, clean-up periods, and seasonal versus permanent working capital lending).

- Refine risk-rating decision making.

- Complete more challenging loan analyses and presentations.

Months Two through Five

■ Learn advanced/detailed aspects of loan analysis (personal financial statements, tax returns, personal cash flow, and breakeven calculation).

■ Refine analysis ability of accrual- versus cash-basis cash flow.

■ Complete still more challenging loan analyses and presentations with more independence.

Months Six through Twelve

■ Learn most advanced aspects of loan analysis (assessing management abilities and business plans, formulating projections and sensitivity analysis, and advanced loan structuring analysis).

■ Learn advanced cash flow analysis and manually construct a statement of cash flows from an income statement and balance sheet.

■ Complete the most difficult loan analyses and presentations.

HOW TO TEACH ANALYSIS OF CASH FLOW

Cash flow analysis is, perhaps, the single most important skill that a successful credit analyst is required to perform. Cash flow analysis is crucial because it is the cash flow of a business that is the **primary** source of repayment for a loan.

In fact, cash flow is the single most important factor in determining whether to approve or renew a loan as well as in determining the loan's risk.

Notice that the training schedule for a new credit analyst revolves around cash flow analysis from week number two until training is complete. For this reason, the department manager and the trainer must be extremely familiar with the concepts of cash flow analysis. The basic aspects of cash flow analysis, including the analysis of the statement of cash flows, are discussed here along with hints for the teaching of cash flow analysis. For detailed analysis techniques, consult *Commercial Loan Analysis* by this author (see Chapter 3 for more information).

Cash Flow Basics

Nearly every bank measures cash flow by constructing a debt service coverage ratio using the "traditional method." Using this method, the analyst begins with net income, adds non-cash expenses such as depreciation, adds interest expense, and adjusts for nonrecurring or nonoperating income or expenses to arrive at a **cash available for debt service** figure. The analyst then divides the cash available figure by the **proposed debt service requirement** to form a **coverage ratio**.

Although the traditional method is extremely useful, it does not represent a complete analysis of cash flow. Because it is based solely on the income statement, the traditional method considers only accrual-based performance and ignores true cash flow. Therefore, to fully analyze cash flow, the statement of cash flows must also be analyzed.

To illustrate accrual versus true cash-basis analysis, consider this example. Assume that a business makes a sale on credit (creating an account receivable), and the business does not receive cash proceeds from the sale until a later date. The proceeds from the sale are not truly available to service debt. However, the traditional method considers all revenues (regardless of when they are collected) as available to service debt.

Conversely, consider a business that incurs an expense this year that it does not actually pay until next year. The traditional method considers this expense to be cash used **this year** and **unavailable** to service this year's debts.

All such sources and uses of cash must be considered to measure true cash flow. This is accomplished by measuring the difference between balance sheet accounts from one period to the next. For example, the difference between the accounts receivable balance this period and the accounts receivable balance at the end of last period represents actual **cash** collected. The statement of cash flows considers all changes in balance sheet items and combines them with income and expenses.

The statement of cash flows is comprised of three sections: operating activities, investing activities, and financing activities. The operating section considers revenues, cost of goods sold, and expenses as does the income statement. This section also considers changes in accounts receivable, accounts payable, inventory, and prepaid and deferred balances between the end of the current period and the end of the previous period.

Because the operating area of the cash flow statement includes these additional factors (referred to as **swing factors**), it should also be the basis of a debt service coverage ratio. A coverage ratio based on the **net cash after operations** line, for example, provides significant additional cash flow information over and above a traditional coverage ratio for the same period.

The investing section of the cash flow statement provides information about capital expenditures and other investing activities. Because it ignores depreciation, this section provides a true measure of cash flow related to fixed asset sales and purchases, which the income statement does not. The financing section illustrates how cash shortfalls are financed or how cash excesses are applied to debt.

Two methods are used to construct cash flow statements. The **direct method** uses a "top-down" approach. A direct statement of cash flows begins with revenue and continues downward to net cash income in a parallel fashion to the income statement. Each accrual measure including revenue, cost of goods sold, and expenses is converted to a cash-basis figure. Because of this, the direct statement can be used to measure cash from sales, gross cash profit, net cash after operations, and net cash income. These values can be compared to historical values and to the corresponding accrual-basis (income statement) figures.

The **indirect method** of reporting cash flow begins with net income and lists all adjustments to convert to cash basis in one section. Since the indirect statement of cash flows begins with net income, it excludes individual measures such as cash from sales and gross cash profit.

Hints for Training Cash Flow Analysis

Because the direct statement is presented in a more familiar format, similar to that of an income statement, it is generally the easier to use for training purposes. In addition, the direct statement is superior for use by the analyst, because it includes performance measures that the indirect statement does not.

To introduce the statement of cash flows to the new analyst it is helpful to explain its similarities and differences to the income statement. Cash flow can be explained in terms of both "sources" and "uses" of cash and in terms of changes in balance sheet accounts from one period to the next.

It is also important to present examples to the analyst who is unclear of the difference between the accrual and the cash basis. For example, if a business makes a cash sale of one dollar, that one dollar represents cash flow, or a source of cash in the amount of one dollar.

Conversely, if the business makes a credit sale of one dollar, and a receivable is created, then no cash is received. To convert the one-dollar sale to the cash basis, the one-dollar receivable that was created must be subtracted from the one-dollar sale, leaving cash flow of zero.

Once the analyst has mastered the basic aspects of cash flow, he or she becomes able to explain swing factors for a given period, which cause cash-basis cash available for debt service to differ from accrual-basis (or traditional) cash available. He or she should begin to communicate and analyze these differences in his or her analysis. At this point, the trainer should recognize this ability or its absence in the analyst. The trainer should then begin to either move into more advanced subjects or review and reinforce cash flow with the analyst.

One advanced subject to include in training is recognition of the underlying reasons for swing factor effects. For example, rapid growth often accompanies increased accounts receivable along with increasing inventories in anticipation of increased sales. These accounts receivable and inventory swing factors represent uses of cash. Therefore, the growing business often experiences cash shortfalls or cash needs (even when cash flow measured by the traditional or accrual basis method appears adequate). The advanced analyst should acquire the ability to recognize the factors which are inherent in cash flow figures.

Finally, an excellent exercise for an advanced analyst is the manual construction of a Statement of Cash Flows from an income statement and a balance sheet provided by the trainer. For the analyst's first try it is good idea to provide assistance; however, the analyst should eventually be able to complete it completely on his or her own. This exercise provides a level of understanding of the Statement of Cash Flows which cannot truly be achieved through instruction alone.

SUMMARY

A formal credit department training program teaches department members to analyze loans accurately, completely, and concisely. A higher-quality work product results. Department member satisfaction also improves since new analysts do not analyze loans before they are ready, and since experienced analysts can be assigned the increased responsibility of involvement in training.

SOURCE

Pirok, Kenneth R. *Commercial Loan Analysis* (Chicago: Probus, 1994).

FIGURE 4–1: FINANCIAL STATEMENT SPREADSHEETS

BALANCE SHEET—ASSETS		
Cash		
Accounts Receivable—Trade		
Less: Allowance for Doubtful Accounts		
Accounts Receivable—Other		
NET ACCOUNTS RECEIVABLE		
Raw Materials		
Work in Progress		
Finished Goods		
Other Inventory		
TOTAL INVENTORY		
Account/Note Receivable		
Income Taxes Receivable		
Prepaid Expenses—Current		
Other Current		
TOTAL CURRENT ASSETS		

FIGURE 4–1 (Continued)

Land		
Buildings		
Furniture and Fixtures		
Machinery and Equipment		
Leasehold Improvements		
Transportation Equipment		
Capitalized Leases		
Other Fixed Assets		
Less: Accumulated Depreciation		
NET FIXED ASSETS		
Account/Note Receivable		
Account/Note Receivable from Officer/Stockholder		
Investments		
Prepaid Expenses		
Cash Value—Life Insurance		
Other Noncurrent Assets		
Intangible Assets		
TOTAL NONCURRENT ASSETS		
TOTAL ASSETS		

FIGURE 4–1 (Continued)

BALANCE SHEET—LIABILITIES/EQUITY		
Overdrafts		
Notes Payable—Short-Term		
Current Portion of Long-Term Debt		
Accounts Payable—Trade		
Accounts Payable—Other		
Account/Note Payable—Officer/Stockholder		
Income Taxes Payable		
Other Current Liabilities		
Accrued Interest		
Dividends Payable		
Accrued Taxes		
Other Accruals		
TOTAL ACCRUED LIABILITIES		
TOTAL CURRENT LIABILITIES		

FIGURE 4–1 (Continued)

Long-Term Debt		
Account/Note Payable—Officer/Stockholder		
Deferred Income Tax		
Deferred Income		
Other Noncurrent Liability		
Subordinate Debt—Liability		
TOTAL NONCURRENT LIABILITIES		
TOTAL LIABILITIES		
Common Stock		
Additional Paid-In Capital		
Less: Treasury Stock		
Retained Earnings		
Other Equity		
TOTAL EQUITY		
TOTAL LIABILITIES AND NET EQUITY		

FIGURE 4–1 (Continued)

INCOME STATEMENT		
Revenue		
Less: Returns and Allowances		
Less: Discounts		
Other Revenue		
NET REVENUE		
Cost of Goods Sold		
Cost of Goods Sold—Other		
Cost of Goods Sold—Depreciation		
TOTAL COST OF GOODS SOLD		
GROSS PROFIT		
Operating Expenses		
Officer Salary		
Rent Expense		
Bad Debt Expense		
Other Operating Expense		
Depreciation Expense		

FIGURE 4–1 (Continued)

Amortization Expense		
TOTAL OPERATING EXPENSE		
OPERATING PROFIT		
Interest Expense		
Interest Income		
Other Expense		
Gain(Loss) on Sale of Assets		
Income Tax		
Extraordinary Gain(Loss)		
OTHER INCOME(EXPENSE)		
NET INCOME		
Dividends		
Accounting Change		
Prior Period Adjustment		
Change in Retained Earnings		
Other Change in Equity		
NET CHANGE IN EQUITY		

Figure 4–1 (Continued)

Statement of Cash Flow		
Net Revenue		
Change in Receivables		
Cash from Revenue		
Cost of Goods Sold		
Change in Inventory		
Change in Accounts Payable		
Cash Production Costs		
Gross Cash Profit		
Operating Expense		
Change in Prepaids		
Change in Accruals		
Cash Operating Expense		
Cash After Operations		
Miscellaneous Cash Income(Expense)		

FIGURE 4–1 (Continued)

Cash Income Tax Paid		
NET CASH AFTER OPERATIONS		
Cash Interest Expense		
NET CASH INCOME		
Current Portion of Long-Term Debt		
CASH AFTER DEBT AMORTIZATION		
Capital Expenditures—Tangible		
Capital Expenditures—Intangible		
FINANCING SURPLUS(DEFICIT)		
Change in Short-Term Debt		
Change in Long-Term Debt		
TOTAL EXTERNAL FINANCING		
Cash After Financing		
Actual Change in Cash		

FIGURE 4–1 (Continued)

PERSONAL ASSETS		
Cash in This Bank		
Cash in Other Banks		
U.S. Government Securities		
Listed Securities		
Other Liquid Assets		
TOTAL LIQUID ASSETS		
Unlisted Securities		
Retirement/IRA		
Inside Business Equity*		
Accounts/Loans Receivable		
Inside Loans Receivable		
Cash Value Life Insurance		
Residence		
Real Estate		
Inside Real Estate*		
Automobiles		
Boat/Aircraft		
Art/Jewelry/Antiques		

FIGURE 4–1 (Continued)

Personal Property/Good		
Personal Property/Question*		
Other Assets		
TOTAL ASSETS		
*Assets marked with star above are excluded from calculation of adjusted net worth.		
PERSONAL LIABILITIES		
Unsecured Loans		
Unsecured Loans		
Secured/Liquid Assets		
Secured/Life Insurance		
Mortgage/Residence		
Mortgage/Real Estate		
Secured/Autos		
Secured/Boat/Plane		
Secured/Other		
Credit Cards		
Taxes Payable		
Other liabilities		
TOTAL LIABILITIES		
TOTAL NET WORTH		

FIGURE 4–1 (Continued)

ADJUSTED NET WORTH		
LIQUID ASSET EQUITY		
LIFE INSURANCE EQUITY		
RESIDENCE EQUITY		
AUTO EQUITY		
PLANE/BOAT EQUITY		

CHAPTER FIVE

LEADING AND MOTIVATING DEPARTMENT MEMBERS

LEADERSHIP

"Leadership" is the ability to influence, persuade, and motivate others toward a certain end. Leadership is an essential quality of the successful credit department manager. To provide effective leadership, it is important that the manager consider the environment and the makeup of the department. Credit department members are professionals, and they should be treated accordingly. For example, department members generally appreciate autonomy along with the ability to request assistance when they feel it is necessary.

Credit department members value the ability to participate in department decision making. A democratic rather than an authoritarian leadership style is more appropriate, since credit department members generally have a great deal of education and experience to offer. In addition, the ability to participate in decision making provides a sense of satisfaction to the participants.

Another aspect of leadership and department member satisfaction is the amount of support that the manager provides. It is important that the credit department manager is available to answer questions, to provide direction, and to listen to his or her department members.

In addition, the manager should support the department's work product and the department's independence. Commercial lenders will frequently disagree with the conclusions or recommendations of the loan analysts. The manager should stand behind the department's analysis and should support the ability of the analysts to present their own conclusions and recommendations. When analysts experience this support, they feel confident in their work product, and more objective and accurate analysis results.

Another aspect of effective leadership is the appropriate use of power. There are various types of power. For example, "coercive power" consists of the manager's ability to punish department members through measures such as suspension or dismissal. The use of coercive power frequently leads to conflict; it should be reserved for serious problems such as chronic tardiness, absenteeism, or insubordination.

"Reward power" consists of the manager's ability to provide positive reinforcement or rewards. The use of this type of power is discussed in the motivation section of this chapter and in the following chapter, which discusses the use of an incentive program.

"Expert power" is derived from experience and knowledge. Expertise in the areas of banking, commercial lending and loan analysis and credit department management are sources of expert power. It is important that the credit department manager be knowledgeable, and it is important that both department members and outsiders feel comfortable in asking him or her for assistance or information.

Chapter 3 details various banking and lending information sources. The following chart details information sources specifically for credit department managers.

NAME OF PUBLICATION	AUTHOR	PUBLISHER/ADDRESS
Bank Management	N/A	Bank Administration Institute Chicago, IL 60606
The Effective Bank Supervisor: Management Skills for Improved Performance (Third Edition)	Paul F. Jannott	Probus Publishing Company Burr Ridge, IL 60521
The Empowered Manager	Peter Block	Jossey-Bass Publishers San Francisco, CA
The Leadership Challenge	James M. Kouzes and Barry Z. Pozner	Jossey-Bass Publishers San Francisco, CA
No Nonsense Management	Andrew Ambraziejus	Longmeadow Press Stamford, CT 06904
13 Fatal Errors Managers Make and How You Can Avoid Them	W. Steven Brown	Berkley Publishing Group New York, NY

NAME OF PUBLICATION	AUTHOR	PUBLISHER/ADDRESS
Common Sense Management and Motivation for the Real World	Roy H. Holmes	Starburst Publishers Lancaster, PA 17604
Bringing Out the Best in People: How to Apply the Astonishing Power of Positive Reinforcement	Aubrey C. Daniels	McGraw-Hill, Inc. New York, NY
What Every Supervisor Should Know (Sixth Edition)	Lester R. Bittel and John W. Newstrom	McGraw-Hill, Inc. New York, NY
The Art of Managing People	Phillip L. Hunsaler and Anthony J. Alessandra	Simon & Schuster, Inc. New York, NY

Finally, power results from the manager's personality. The manager's ability to remain enthusiastic, to persuade, to handle conflict, and to motivate constitute "personality power."

The effective credit department manager must handle conflict among department members as well as between department members and himself or herself. Various strategies for handling conflict are useful in certain situations.

It is appropriate to act in a quick and/or decisive manner when the manager knows the correct action or when unpopular action must be taken. Compromise or consensus should be encouraged to solve complicated issues, issues for which a correct solution is not apparent, and issues arising when the arguments of all conflicting parties are valid. In addition, compromise or consensus are appropriate when bad feelings are likely to result from choosing to support one of the parties. Finally, it is appropriate to avoid issues that are trivial or unimportant in comparison with other issues. It is also appropriate to delay the settlement of issues when additional information is required or when the conflicting parties need time to relax.

Motivation

People are motivated by various needs. The successful credit department manager identifies and satisfies the needs of the department members in order motivate them. For example, basic needs include food, clothing, shelter, and healthcare. These basic needs are satisfied through compensation and benefits.

However, in addition to basic needs, people have advanced types of needs such as self-esteem and happiness. These needs are satisfied through recognition, responsibility, achievement, and variety. It is essential that the credit department manager recognizes which of these needs are important to individual department members and that he or she satisfies these needs. The following chapter discusses satisfaction of needs through the institution of an incentive program.

In addition, there are various methods to motivate department members without the use of compensation or incentives. For example, an enthusiastic department manager and a manager who sets a good example creates a great deal of motivation simply as a result of his or her attitude.

SOURCES

Daft, Richard L. *Management* (Chicago: The Dryden Press, 1988), 366–424.

Robbins, Stephen P. *Organizational Behavior,* 4th ed. (Englewood Cliffs, N.J.: Prentice Hall, 1989), 301–395.

Thomas, K.W. "Conflict and Conflict Management." *Handbook of Industrial and Organizational Psychology* (Chicago: Rand McNally, 1976), 889–935.

Thomas, K.W. "Toward Multidimensional Values in Teaching: The Example of Conflict Behaviors." *Academy of Management Review* (July 1977), 487.

CHAPTER SIX

HOW TO INSTITUTE AN INCENTIVE PROGRAM

The institution of an incentive system improves the credit department by promoting and reinforcing better performance from each member. the use of incentives results not only in a higher-quality work product but in more satisfied department members. The costs of such a program are relatively small; any costs of incentives are recovered through improved performance.

USING GOALS AND INCENTIVES

Determine What to Measure

The objective of the incentive system is to recognize and reward performance. In order to recognize performance, one must first determine exactly what to measure.

Two measures of performance are quantity and quality of work produced. There is an inverse relationship between these two measures. As the quantity of work produced increases over a given period of time, the quality of the work product decreases, and vice versa. These factors must be weighed, and a priority must be established.

Commercial loan analysis is important to the bank because it provides the basis upon which loan decisions are made. Accurate loan decisions are crucial to bank performance. Because of this, the quality of loan analysis is also crucial. It is more important to have an accurate and complete analysis than to have the analysis available immediately. Therefore, measuring loan analysis quality is considered a higher priority than measuring quantity produced over time.

It is also important to maximize the use of measurements that are tangible, easily measured, and objective, and it is important to minimize the use of those that are difficult to measure or are subjective in nature. This allows clarity concerning what constitutes good performance, and it also results in the feeling that the analyst actually controls his or her own performance level.

Finally, seniority should not be considered when measuring performance or when rewarding department members.

Seniority is considered indirectly, since greater experience leads to more accurate, complete, and timely analyses, and since it is the measurement of these factors that determines rewards. It is unfair to reward two employees differently, based on seniority, if they perform equally well.

Set Goals

Once you have determined what to measure, goals should be set for each department member. It is the achievement of goals that is rewarded by incentives. Goals should be set above the standard level of performance; therefore, if goals are met, improvement in the individual and in the department occurs.

Goals should be realistic and attainable. If a goal is unnecessarily high, then an attempt to achieve it will probably not even be made. Each department member should participate in goal setting. This process provides each member with a sense of control over his or her destiny, a sense of ownership and pride in work produced, and a knowledge of what is expected and what is important (Belasco, 1990, 115).

Provide Feedback

Feedback should be provided as soon as possible each time an analyst's work is evaluated; it should occur while the analysis is still fresh in the minds of both the analyst and the evaluator. Feedback allows the analyst to be aware of strengths and weaknesses, and it allows him or her to improve on areas of poor performance and to maintain areas of strength. Most importantly, frequent and complete feedback provides a feeling that the analyst controls the quality of his or her work.

Feedback should consist of actual discussion, and an understanding should be reached with the analyst concerning the quality of his or her work. Discussion is especially important when measurements of work quality are subjective in nature because, in this case, the underlying reasons behind a subjective evaluation are not apparent to the analyst without an explanation.

Provide Incentives

Incentives should be discussed during goal setting. Specific incentives should be matched with the achievement of specific goals. This provides the motivation to achieve each goal.

There are various types of incentives, each of which can be extremely effective. One category consists of the short-term incentive. This category includes incentives such as a day or a half-day away from work, a free lunch or dinner, a reserved parking space, flowers, candy, or tickets to sporting or theater events. Such incentives are used to reward smaller, shorter-term goals. Short-term incentives can be extremely successful since the rewards usually directly create enjoyment for the person being rewarded and because the reward is easily tied to the achievement by which it was preceded in the mind of the person being rewarded.

Another type of incentive consists of recognition or awards. A weekly or monthly award can be a great motivator. The author once had a swim coach who gave out a Tootsie Roll each time a swimmer beat his previous best time in a given event. These awards were given weekly in front of the entire team, and they truly motivated the swimmers. However, it was not the Tootsie Rolls that motivated the swimmer, but it was the recognition that was the true reward. This shows that merely being recognized and encouraging a feeling of self-worth is as important, or more important, than the tangible incentive itself.

The strongest incentives are compensation increases and promotions. Such rewards should, therefore, be tied to the achievement of multiple long-term goals. The concept of "pay-for-performance" should be the most important aspect of credit analyst compensation; however, the use of compensation as an incentive is, perhaps, the most overlooked method of improving analyst performance.

An unfortunate reality is that compensation increases or promotions are not always available to be offered by the credit department. In this case, increases in responsibility are also an excellent incentive. A great feeling of self-worth and satisfaction results when an analyst gains increased responsibility. Examples of increased responsibility for credit analysts might include guest membership to a loan committee, ability to attend customer calls, ability to analyze larger loan relationships, or the ability to train and evaluate newer analysts.

HOW TO MEASURE PERFORMANCE

Accuracy

Since accuracy is a crucial, if not the most crucial, aspect of commercial loan analysis, the accuracy of various elements of loan analysis is measured for use in employee evaluations.

Specifically, the accuracy of financial statement spreads, cash flow and financial analyses, and collateral analyses can be measured and reported.

The supervisor should examine completed spreads to ensure that all accounts are classified appropriately. Cash flow and financial analyses should be examined to determine that all values and all ratios are reported correctly. Results should be reported for evaluation purposes, and any mistakes uncovered should be communicated to the analyst for correction and for avoidance in the future.

The supervisor will frequently not have time available to examine every spreadsheet or every cash flow analysis that an analyst completes. In this case, the supervisor should examine analyses periodically. The findings, along with resulting improvement (or lack of improvement) in the analyst's work, can be used for evaluation.

In addition, the supervisor can develop a series of increasingly complex assignments. The analyst's performance can be measured by his or her ability to complete each successive assignment accurately.

It should be noted that accuracy can only be measured in relation to established bank or department policies and procedures. Policy must dictate a method for completion of analysis and describe a style for reporting the results. Further, the policy is only as good as the extent to which it is communicated to and understood by the analysts.

For example, many banks consider prepaid expenses and officer or employee receivables to be noncurrent or intangible assets regardless of their classification in the raw financial statements. The bank's policy for such asset classification should be communicated to the analyst so that he or she may spread financial statements accordingly. With such knowledge, the analyst can be held responsible for preparing accurate spreadsheets, reported in the manner required by the bank.

At many banks, analysts propose appropriate loan ratings for relationships that they analyze. The accuracy of these proposed loan ratings can also be used as a measure of performance. Although loan ratings are somewhat subjective, a consensus concerning the correct rating can usually be achieved. The analyst's ability to defend his or her proposed loan rating with relevant factors should be the most important measurement concerning loan rating accuracy.

Completeness

Completeness is also a very important aspect of commercial loan analysis. A single factor may mean the difference between approval and denial; if this factor is omitted from the analysis, then the wrong decision may be made. The analyst's ability to minimize relevant items that are omitted from analyses should, therefore, be measured.

Completeness can be measured by the supervisor and by other analysts who check that all major issues are addressed and that the few most important issues are listed clearly in the write-up or analysis summary. Another measure consists of tracking major issues, brought up during loan committee discussion, that had been omitted from write-ups.

Concise Analysis

Concise analysis is important for two reasons. First, loan officers and loan committee members operate on tight schedules, and they need only the major, relevant factors to make loan decisions in a timely manner. Second, overly extensive loan analysis wastes time that can be spent on other projects. Therefore, analysis should also be examined to see that it remains short and to the point.

Advanced Analysis and Supervision

As analysts gain experience, more advanced measurements become necessary. A typical requirement for a new credit analyst to advance to the next level is the ability to manually construct a statement of cash flows from a balance sheet and an income statement.

The performance of the supervisor or trainer should be based on the ability and improvement of his or her subordinates or trainees in providing accurate, complete, and concise analyses.

Any supervisor or trainer whose individual performance is measured by the performance of others should, however, have the authority, the resources, and the time available to work with subordinates or trainees. The proper authority must exist to match the responsibility of providing training. For example, the trainer needs the authority to assign work and to test the analysts. The supervisor or trainer must be able to teach and to change the abilities of the analysts to be judged fairly by those analyst's abilities.

Implementation and Results

Your bank should institute an incentive program. Such a program only has a cost to the bank if credit analyst performance improves. If performance is improved, then costs are recovered through increased productivity, increased satisfaction, and most importantly through more accurate loan decisions resulting from more accurate analysis.

Source

Belasco, Kent S. *Bank Productivity: Improving Performance by Managing Non-Interest Expense* (Chicago: Probus Publishing Company, 1990).

CHAPTER SEVEN

ADDITIONAL SERVICES THE CREDIT DEPARTMENT CAN OFFER

The credit department can offer the bank a wide variety of services in addition to the traditional task of commercial loan analysis. The department can be especially beneficial when an extra degree of organization or control is necessary.

CREDIT INQUIRIES

Banks frequently exchange credit information with other banks and with trade creditors of commercial borrowers. For example, a supplier of a commercial borrower may inquire about the borrower's repayment history to the bank to determine whether it wishes to supply its product to the borrower on credit. The exchange of such credit information is an important task that can be performed by the credit department. The use of the credit department ensures accuracy, promptness, and organization as well as full use of information obtained through the process.

It is extremely important to answer credit inquiries accurately. Accuracy is important because the inquirer makes a credit decision based on the information received. An improper answer could impair the ability of a business (usually a bank customer) to purchase inventory or a fixed asset. This could, in turn, lead to the inability of the bank customer to repay the bank. An improper or incomplete answer even subjects the bank to potential liability.

Credit department members understand the need for accurate credit information, so they are an excellent choice to answer credit inquiries. Robert Morris Associates publishes a *Code of Ethics for the Exchange of Commercial Credit Information between Banks*. This code governs credit inquiries made by banks to other banks. Robert Morris Associates and the National Association of Credit Management publish a *Statement of Principles for the Exchange of Credit Information between Banks and Business Credit Grantors*. This code governs credit inquiries made by trade creditors to banks. The use of these standards for training and reference is important to ensure accurate response to inquiries and to limit bank liability. These publications can be obtained from Robert Morris Associates at the address or phone number in Chapter 3.

Promptness is important because a business could lose the opportunity to make a purchase with special terms offered for only a limited time. Organization is important to ensure that no inquiries are lost and that inquiries are filed properly for subsequent referral or for further use by the bank. Since promptness and organization are also typical traits of the credit department, its members can be used to answer credit inquiries.

Although nearly every bank answers credit inquiries, the process is often overlooked as a means of obtaining information about the bank's commercial borrowers. Through credit inquiries, the bank learns about potential capital purchases, the use of suppliers, and even about potential refinances at other banks by its commercial loan customers. The credit department can be used to place inquiries in credit files, and it can be responsible for alerting loan officers of any important information learned through the exchange of credit information.

CONTROL OVER APPROVED LOANS

The credit department can be used to control loan disbursements. To ensure that all loans have the proper approval, the credit department can be made responsible for securing signatures of the individual loan officers or of the committee members who approve a loan. Further, department members can verify that the approving body does, indeed, have the authority to approve the loan and that the loan relationship fits within legal lending limits. The credit department should then provide proof of proper approval to the person or department that prepares the loan documents and to whomever provides loan funds.

A sample loan approval worksheet form (Figure 7–1) appears at the end of this chapter. This worksheet is used as a cover sheet to the loan presentation, which is placed in the credit file after approval. This worksheet should also be filed along with a copy of the minutes for loans that are presented verbally to a committee. In addition to providing documentation of proper approval to anyone who examines the file, this form should be provided to the person preparing the loan documents and providing the funds.

DOCUMENTATION REVIEW

The credit department can also be made responsible for loan documentation review. The department member can prepare a checklist of required and/or suggested loan documents for each approved loan. He or she can also perform periodic file reviews to verify that ongoing documentation is sufficient. Sample commercial loan documentation checklists appear at the end of this chapter (Figures 7–2, 7–3, and 7–4).

In addition, the credit department can be responsible for tracking financial statements and other loan information. The department member can date-stamp or date and initial each document when it is received and file it appropriately. Credit department members may also keep a current list of documentation exceptions and check them off when they are satisfied. Exception tracking may include the use of a tickler system, which alerts the bank to financial statements, insurance renewals, or UCC filing renewals that need to be acted on.

Financial statement tracking is an important aspect of loan documentation because receipt of statements is an ongoing process. Credit department members can organize a system to track receipt of statements, and they can be relied on to request statements from borrowers when statements are late or absent. Upon receipt, credit analysts generally spread the statements and file them appropriately.

In various states, in order for the bank to rely on accountant-prepared financial statements, a "reliance letter" must be received by the bank from the preparer. A reliance letter should be received from the accountant each time reviewed or audited financial statements are prepared. This allows the bank to hold the accountant liable for inaccurate financial statement figures. (Consult with bank counsel to determine whether reliance letters are required in your particular state and for help in constructing a letter to be signed by accountants.) The credit department can be made responsible for contacting accountants and for ensuring that reliance letters are received. (The reliance letter is included as a line item on the loan documentation review forms at the end of this chapter.)

Including the credit department in the loan documentation process provides an extra check to ensure that any required or preferred documentation is performed and updated. It also ensures that documentation conforms to loan policy and to the exact structure which was approved. A final advantage is that responsibility for loan documentation provides the credit analyst with excellent experience for a career in commercial lending.

CREDIT FILE AND NOTE ADMINISTRATION

The credit department can even be made responsible for maintaining the credit files and for checking files and notes in and out. Credit department members frequently have more time available than loan officers to organize credit files. Also, members can use a uniform filing method so that files remain organized and so that documents are easy to find. Working with the files also provides excellent exposure to commercial lending and loan documentation.

The use of credit department members to check loan files and/or notes in and out provides an extra degree of control and security over files and notes. With a formal check-out procedure, lost files can be minimized since documentation always exists concerning who has the file.

RELATIONSHIP PROFITABILITY ANALYSIS

The credit department may be responsible for relationship profitability analysis. This process involves collecting bank-specific data and goals and measuring whether each individual commercial customer is profitable to the bank. The use of profitability analysis is also a tool for the pricing of proposed loans.

Profitability analysis involves the use of formulas that can be calculated manually or with a spreadsheet program such as Lotus 1-2-3. As an alternative, various software firms offer pricing model software that automates the profitability analysis process (Altenbernd 1994, 83):

COMMERCIAL LOAN PRICING MODEL SOFTWARE	ADDRESS/PHONE
FAST Pricer	Financial Proformas, Inc. 1855 Olympic Avenue, Suite 200 Walnut Creek, CA 94596 (510) 945-1005
Bank Performance System	Profit Management Associates 1295 Idylberry Road San Rafael, CA 94903 (415) 472-3210
Credit Officer's Pricing Evaluator (COPE)	Nortridge Software P. O. Box 598 Freeport, IL 61032 (800) 435-7240
PRICE	Baker Hill Corporation 655 West Carmel Drive, Suite 100 Carmel, IN 46032 (800) 821-2220
Loan Pricing/Customer Profitability	James Baker & Company 1601 Northwest Expressway, #2000 Oklahoma City, OK 73118 (405) 842-1400
Toprate	Copeland Financial Group 22 East Poplar Walla Walla, Washington 99362 (509) 522-0900
Relationship Analysis Program	Vantage Financial Group & American Bankers Association 1120 Connecticut Avenue, N.W. Washington, DC 20036 (800) 338-0626

The primary advantage of the use of loan pricing software over manual and Lotus 1-2-3 calculation is that pricing software is able to make much more sophisticated calculations than can be performed easily by hand or through the use of a spreadsheet. For example, variables such as unused commitments, loan and deposit fees, variable rates, reserve requirements, bank balance sheet leverage, bank overhead, and costs of funds should all factor into loan pricing; however, manual calculations become extremely complex as more of these variables are considered.

A sample pricing analysis for a commercial loan and deposit relationship (Figure 7–5) appears at the end of this chapter. This analysis was produced by the American Bankers Association's Relationship Analysis Program, and it includes both the data input into the program by the analyst and the data output by the program.

RISK RATING

The credit department may offer the service of tracking and reporting commercial loan risk ratings and/or recommendation of appropriate ratings in loan analysis. Risk rating is an important aspect of loan analysis and reporting. Because of this, it is important that the analysts become familiar with the bank's risk-rating system by recommending ratings. In addition, the department's organizational skills can be tapped by making the credit department responsible for tracking and reporting the ratings. To support both the choosing and reporting of risk ratings, a few firms offer software to automate the process.

The bank's criteria for choosing the appropriate risk rating are generally reported in the loan policy. A typical rating system has nine categories of risk-ratings. A sample risk rating system is as follows:

Risk Rating 1

General Description:	Loans to large and strong borrowers (generally publicly traded companies operating nationwide or globally) with the highest debt ratings, loans secured by deposits or adequately margined, marketable securities, or loans guaranteed by the federal government or an agency of the federal government such as the Small Business Administration.
Cash Flow/ Income Statement:	Generally, significantly greater than 1.2:1 debt service coverage with a long history.
Balance Sheet:	Generally, leverage and liquidity are significantly more favorable than industry averages, and operating/turnover ratios are similar or more favorable than industry averages.
Financial Statement Quality:	Audited by a Big Six accounting firm.

Collateral:

Frequently, loans to large/strong borrowers are unsecured.

Additional Support:

Generally, none is necessary.

Loan Documentation:

No significant flaws.

Management Ability:

Management ability is excellent, and succession is in place.

Industrial/Business/ Competitive/ Economic Analysis:

Firm operates in a strong and growing or stable industry, which is not cyclical in nature, and the firm has no sales concentrations to any one customer.

Risk Rating 2

General Description:

Loans to strong, national, or regional borrowers with relatively high debt ratings or loans secured by adequately margined, marketable securities (of less quality or liquidity than for loans rated 1).

Cash Flow/Income Statement:

Generally, significantly greater than 1.2:1 debt service coverage with a long history.

Balance Sheet:

Generally, leverage and liquidity are more favorable than industry averages, and operating/turnover ratios are similar or more favorable than industry averages.

Financial Statement Quality:	Audited.
Collateral:	Frequently, loans to strong borrowers are unsecured.
Additional Support:	Generally, none is necessary.
Loan Documentation:	No significant flaws.
Management Ability:	Management ability is excellent, and succession is in place.
Industrial/Business/ Competitive/ Economic Analysis:	Firm operates in a strong and growing or stable industry, which is not significantly cyclical in nature, and the firm has no large concentrations of sales to any one customer.

Risk Rating 3

General Description:	Loans to relatively strong borrowers (generally operating on a local or regional basis).
Cash Flow/ Income Statement:	Generally, debt service coverage is 1.2:1 or greater. Debt service coverage and profits exhibit upward trends and/or a history of a few years.
Balance Sheet:	Generally leverage, liquidity, and operating/turnover ratios compare favorably to industry averages.

Financial Statement Quality:	Audited, reviewed, or tax returns (externally prepared).
Collateral:	Collateral coverage is sufficient and falls within loan policy norms.
Additional Support:	Personal guarantees or personal co-borrowers as well as assignments of life insurance are frequently necessary.
Loan Documentation:	No significant flaws.
Management Ability:	Management ability is good. Management is trusted, and succession or life insurance is in place.
Industrial/Business/ Competitive/ Economic Analysis:	Firm generally operates in a strong and growing or stable industry, which is not significantly cyclical in nature, and the firm has no large concentrations of sales to any one customer.

Risk Rating 4

General Description:	Loans to relatively strong borrowers with some added degree of risk (requiring additional monitoring). Any one of the weaknesses below may be reason for inclusion in this category.
Cash Flow/ Income Statement:	Generally, debt service coverage approximates or falls just short of

1.2:1. Debt service coverage and profits may be stable, or they may trend downward.

Balance Sheet:

Leverage, liquidity, and operating/turnover ratios fall slightly below industry averages.

Financial Statement Quality:

Compiled, internally prepared, or tax returns.

Collateral:

Collateral coverage falls within or marginally below loan policy norms.

Additional Support:

Personal guarantees or personal co-borrowers as well as assignments of life insurance are frequently necessary. Lack of necessary guarantees or insurance may be reasons for inclusion in this category.

Loan Documentation:

Financial statements outdated or hazard insurance expired.

Management Ability:

Management is trusted, but may not be entirely successful or able.

Industrial/Business/ Competitive/ Economic Analysis:

Firm is in stable or declining industry, which may be cyclical in nature. The firm may have significant concentrations of sales to a single or a few customers; the firm may be a recent start-up. Real estate or hotels may show some vacancy, or they may have experienced rent concessions, construction delays, or a change in concept such as condominiums converting to apartments.

Risk Rating 5—"Watch"

General Description:

Loans with added risk requiring more significant monitoring; however, eventual collection of loans in this category is not in serious doubt. Any one of the weaknesses below may be reason for inclusion in this category.

Cash Flow/Income Statement:

Generally, debt service coverage approximates or falls slightly short of 1:1. Debt service coverage and profits generally unfavorable or trend downward.

Balance Sheet:

Leverage, liquidity, and operating/turnover ratios fall below industry averages. Firms in this category may have a small deficit equity position.

Financial Statement Quality:

Compiled, internally prepared, or tax returns.

Collateral:

Collateral coverage falls below loan policy norms. A slight short-

	fall would result if collateral were liquidated.
Additional Support:	Personal guarantees or personal co-borrowers as well as assignments of life insurance are usually necessary; however, guarantees frequently provide no additional support. Lack of necessary guarantees or insurance may be reasons for inclusion in this category.
Loan Documentation:	Financial statements outdated.
Management Ability:	Management may be mistrusted and/or may not be entirely successful or able.
Industrial/Business/ Competitive/ Economic Analysis:	Firm is in declining industry, which may be cyclical in nature, and the firm may have a significant concentration of sales to a single or a few customers. Real estate or hotels show significant vacancy, or they may have experienced serious rent concessions, construction delays, or a change in concept such as condominiums converting to apartments.

Risk Rating 6—"Other Assets Especially Mentioned (OAEM)"

General Description:	Loans with added risk requiring significant monitoring due to po-

tential weaknesses. Eventual collection of loans in this category remains probable, and delinquencies may not have occurred yet. Any one of the weaknesses below may be reason for inclusion in this category.

Cash Flow/Income Statement:

Debt service coverage falls short of 1:1 or may be undeterminable. Debt service coverage and profits are unfavorable (losses are common) or trend downward.

Balance Sheet:

Leverage, liquidity, and operating/turnover ratios fall significantly below industry averages. Firms in this category are frequently insolvent.

Financial Statement Quality:

Internally prepared statements believed to be inaccurate, or statements may not be provided at all.

Collateral:

Collateral coverage falls below loan policy norms. A shortfall would result if collateral were liquidated.

Additional Support:

Personal guarantees or personal co-borrowers as well as assignments of life insurance are usually necessary; however, guarantees fre-

	quently provide no additional support.
Loan Documentation:	Financial statements outdated; loan agreement inadequate; validity of mortgage in doubt; or UCC filing expired.
Management Ability:	Management may be mistrusted and/or may not be entirely successful or able. The firm may have experienced bad publicity, which could adversely affect future debt service ability.
Industrial/Business/ Competitive/ Economic Analysis:	Firm is in declining industry or geographic area. Real estate or hotels show significant vacancy, or they may have experienced serious rent concessions, construction delays, or a change in concept such as condominiums converting to apartments.

Risk Rating 7—"Substandard"

General Description:	Full collection of loans in this category become doubtful due to inadequate cash flow, collateral, and/or additional support. Loans in this category generally do not accrue interest.

Cash Flow/Income
Statement:

Debt service coverage falls significantly short of 1:1, and payments are usually delinquent. Firms in this category are rarely profitable.

Balance Sheet:

Leverage, liquidity, and operating/turnover ratios fall significantly below industry averages. Firms in this category are usually insolvent and/or bankrupt.

Financial Statement
Quality:

Internally prepared statements may be believed to be inaccurate, or statements may not be provided at all.

Collateral:

A shortfall would result if collateral were liquidated.

Additional Support:

Guarantees usually provide no additional support.

Loan Documentation:

Validity of mortgage may be in doubt, or a UCC filing may be expired. The loan documentation weakness leads the bank to doubt the full collectibility of the loan.

Management Ability:

Management may be mistrusted and/or may not be successful or able.

Industrial/Business/
Competitive/
Economic Analysis:

Firm is in declining industry. Major customers or tenants may have been lost. Real estate or hotels show significant vacancy. Construction may have ceased.

Risk Rating 8—"Doubtful"

General Description: Collection of loans in this category are doubtful; however, the amount of loss that the bank expects to incur cannot yet be determined. Loans generally do not accrue interest, and a specific allocation may be necessary.

Cash Flow/Income Statement: Debt service coverage falls significantly short of 1:1. Firms in this category are rarely profitable.

Balance Sheet: Leverage, liquidity, and operating/turnover ratios fall significantly below industry averages. Firms in this category are usually insolvent and/or bankrupt.

Financial Statement Quality: Internally prepared statements believed to be inaccurate, or statements may not be provided at all.

Collateral: A significant shortfall would result if collateral were liquidated.

Additional Support: No additional support is provided.

Loan Documentation: Validity of mortgage may be in doubt, or a UCC filing may be expired. The loan documentation weakness leads the bank to doubt the collectibility of the loan.

Management Ability: Management is mistrusted and/or may not be successful or able.

Industrial/Business/ Competitive/ Economic Analysis: Firm is in declining industry. Major customers or tenants may have been lost. Real estate or hotels show significant vacancy. Construction may have ceased.

Risk Rating 9—"Loss"

General Description: A loss has been determined for loans in this category, and the uncollectible amount has been charged-off.

PREPARING FOR BANK EXAMS

All financial institutions are examined regularly by an agency of the government such as the Office of the Comptroller of the Currency (OCC), the Federal Reserve, or the Federal Deposit Insurance Corporation (FDIC). An examination consists of an evaluation of a bank's safety, soundness, and compliance with regulations. The examining agency also assigns the bank a composite rating according to the following broad definitions (Comptroller of the Currency, 1989, 17):

1. Bank is basically sound in every respect; critical findings or comments are of a minor nature and can be handled in a routine manner.

2. Bank is fundamentally sound, but has weaknesses that are correctable in the normal course of business.

3. Bank exhibits combinations of financial, operational, or compliance weaknesses that range from moderately severe to unsatisfactory.

4. Bank has an immoderate volume of serious financial weaknesses or a combination of other conditions that are unsatisfactory.

5. Bank has an extremely high immediate or near-term probability of failure.

The credit department has a role in preparing for examination by the bank's regulating agency. The department's primary function is typically that of an information gatherer and distributor. Department members gather bank loan policy, department loan policy, standard commercial lending forms and documents, risk-rating reports, legal lending limit aggregation and reports, and SIC code and concentration reports, and the department provides this information to the examiners.

Credit department members can also be used to gather specific credit files requested by the examiners. Department members can be responsible for checking files in and out and for making sure that files are organized and returned to the proper place after use by the examiners.

It is important to know that the examiners will ask questions of credit department members. It is crucial that department members be prepared to answer such questions. It is also crucial that department members refer both sensitive questions and questions that they do not know how to answer to the supervisor.

The department should meet as a group before the examination to discuss frequently asked questions and to define questions that should be referred to the supervisor. Department members should feel comfortable discussing basic department operating procedures with the examiners. Examiners receive an extra degree of comfort with the bank when they observe sound commercial loan analysis and administration procedures and when they observe credit department members who understand and act according to the procedures.

WORKING WITH INTERNAL LOAN REVIEW

Members of the internal loan review department perform tasks such as analysis of loan loss reserve sufficiency, auditing of loan reports and procedures for report preparation, auditing of files to ensure adequate documentation and analysis, maintenance of risk ratings, analysis and reporting on the quality of the loan portfolio, and measurement of adherence by lenders to loan policy. The credit department works closely with the loan review department, and many tasks performed by the credit department are shared with loan review. In addition, loan reviewers typically audit the work of credit department members as well as that of the entire lending area.

In order to support the loan review function, the credit department must provide loan review personnel with various types of reports and information. It is important to maintain a level of openness with loan review so that its members can correctly assess the loan reporting and approval processes as well as the quality of the loan portfolio. The credit department can act as an information gatherer for loan review by compiling reports or by retrieving files or approval presentations. Credit department members may even train loan review members on loan analysis topics. Such training allows loan review to maximize the effectiveness of its reviews and provides loan review with comfort and confidence regarding the level of analysis that is performed as well as with the skills of the analysts.

MERGERS AND ACQUISITIONS

When banks consolidate, the credit department also has an important role. The credit department typically acts as an information gatherer and distributor in a similar manner to that of preparing for bank examinations or loan review. In addition to providing bank policies and reports, department members may gather local economic and real estate analysis as well as specific industry analyses to provide background information for the new banking partner.

The credit department may also present its analysis methods, policies and procedures, standard reporting formats, and examples to new credit department members or commercial lending department members. A great deal of communication and training are necessary during consolidation in order to minimize new department members' problems adjusting and to minimize any slowdown in the turnover of department work.

In addition, compassion is important during restructuring toward those department members who are losing their positions or who are being relocated to a new physical location or to a different department within the bank. The department manager has the responsibility to encourage sensitivity during restructuring. The use of humor and the practice of stress-management techniques such as relaxation at work and exercise at home are additional ways to alleviate tension during restructuring. Another resource is Pritchett & Associates, Inc., an organization that provides various training manuals, books, and seminars for businesses undergoing organizational change.[1]

It is important to note that techniques for dealing with organizational change such as communication, compassion, sensitivity, humor, stress management, and training seminars are the same techniques to use when starting up or reorganizing the credit department. The commercial lending department will typically be concerned and even resistant about the idea of using the credit department to analyze loans, to organize files, or to provide loan reporting. When the lending area gives responsibility to the credit depart-

---

1 Pritchett & Associates is located at 13155 Noel Road, Suite 1600, Dallas, Texas; (800) 622-8989.

ment, a significant organizational change occurs. Dealing with this change requires communication, compassion, and the other change-management techniques described above.

LOAN COMMITTEE MINUTES

The minutes of loan committee meetings are commonly prepared and centrally filed by a member of the credit department. Designation of a credit department member as secretary of the loan committee has various advantages. The secretary is forced to pay close attention to loan committee discussions, and, through observation of the committee and preparation of the minutes, he or she learns a great deal about the approval process and about each loan relationship presented to the committee.

In addition, designation of a credit department member as Secretary allows a control process to occur. The secretary can be responsible for ensuring that the exact loan structure approved during the meeting is presented in the minutes and is used in the actual loan documentation.

Accuracy is an important aspect of loan committee minutes. The secretary should take notes during the committee meeting, and he or she should use these notes to prepare a draft of the minutes. The credit department manager and/or the committee chairperson should review the draft for accuracy before the minutes are finalized.

In addition, the minutes must be complete, with all important information from the committee meeting included. The following items should generally be included in the minutes:

- Committee name

- Date of meeting

- Committee members and guests present

- Committee members absent

- Details of each approved loan, including:

  Loan request

  Purpose

  Pricing

  Repayment terms

  Collateral

  Additional support

  Controls

  Conditions of approval

  Exceptions to policy

  Risk rating

  Total dollar amount of relationship

- Other business

- Signatures of committee chairperson and secretary

Finally, as a precaution, all printed loan committee minutes should be locked in a fireproof cabinet or vault, and computer files of the minutes should be backed up periodically and stored at an alternate site. These measures provide back-up in the event of disaster as well as a control feature, which reduces the likelihood that minutes can be altered.

LOAN LOSS RESERVE SUFFICIENCY ANALYSIS

Sufficient loan loss reserves are crucial to the bank. The credit department can support loan loss reserve sufficiency analysis through the tracking and reporting of delinquencies, risk ratings, loan volume, portfolio concentrations, and charge-offs.

Specifically, the credit department can report historical trends in delinquencies, loan volume, and portfolio concentrations and their effects on charge-offs. Credit department members can also report historical charge-offs categorized by risk rating as well as maintain a migration analysis of charge-offs, and they can report on the real estate market and the economy. Using these reports, bank management can accurately analyze loan loss reserve sufficiency. The following publications address loan loss reserves and the factors impacting reserves:

TITLE	AUTHOR	PUBLISHER
Banking Circular 201	Comptroller of the Currency	Office of the Comptroller of the Currency (202) 874-5170
Allowance for Loan and Lease Losses for Community Banks	Robert Morris Associates	Robert Morris Associates (800) 677-7621

TITLE	AUTHOR	PUBLISHER
"Maintaining the Allowance for Loan Losses: A Prescription for the 1990s" *Commercial Lending Review* (Winter 1990–91)	John K. Fletcher and Harriet S. Wassertrum	John Colet Press and American Bankers Association (800) 338-0626
"Regulatory Update: The Evolution of the Allowance for Loan and Lease Losses" *Commercial Lending Review* (Fall 1994)	Christie A. Sciacca	Institutional Investor, Inc. and American Bankers Association (800) 338-0626
"Managing Credit Concentrations: Policies and Practices for Achieving Balanced Portfolios," *Commercial Lending Review* (Fall 1994)	Bruce G. Stevenson	Institutional Investor, Inc. and American Bankers Association (800) 338-0626
"How to Make Migration Analysis Work for You" *The Journal of Commercial Lending* (November 1994)	John W. Gleason	Robert Morris Associates (800) 677-7621
Interagency Policy Statement on the Allowance for Loan and Lease Losses	Federal Deposit Insurance Corporation and financial institution regulatory agencies	Contact your institution's regulatory agency for information.

SUMMARY

The credit department can offer a wide variety of services and support to the commercial lending function. Since the department's strengths typically include organization, control, and accuracy, it can be used for tasks requiring these skills. It is important for the department manager and for department members to realize that as more reporting and monitoring tasks are added to the department's workload, the level of responsibility of the department increases, time management becomes important, and techniques for handling organizational change become important.

SOURCES

A Director's Guide to Board Reports. Office of the Comptroller of the Currency (July 1989).

Altenbernd, Mark. "What Should Loan Pricing Software Do for You?" *Commercial Lending Review*, Vol. 9, No. 2 (Spring 1994), 80–84.

Comptroller's Handbook for National Bank Examiners. Office of the Comptroller of the Currency (March 1990), Section 215.1, 1–2.

Gleason, John W. "How to Make Migration Analysis Work for You." *The Journal of Commercial Lending*, Vol. 77, No. 3 (November 1994), 16–25.

Hoffman, Margaret A., and Fischer, Gerald C. *Credit Department Management* (Philadelphia: Robert Morris Associates, 1980), 59–65, 133–120.

N.A. Loan Policy: Allowance for Loan Losses. First Midwest Bank/Danville (December 1993).

N.A. Loan Policy: Loan Risk Ratings. First Midwest Bank/Danville (May 19, 1994).

Schatz, Edward K. "New People, Policies, and Places: How to Manage a Credit Department Merger." *The Journal of Commercial Lending* (February 1994), 26–31.

Sciacca, Christie A. "Regulatory Update: The Evolution of the Allowance for Loan and Lease Losses." *Commercial Lending Review*, Vol. 9, No. 4 (Fall 1994) 87–91.

Stevenson, Bruce G. "Managing Credit Concentrations: Policies and Practices for Achieving Balanced Portfolios." *Commercial Lending Review,* Vol. 9, No. 4 (Fall 1994), 14–23.

Ullom, Robert V. *How to Audit a Loan File.* Seminar sponsored by St. Louis American Institute of Banking.

FIGURE 7–1: LOAN APPROVAL WORKSHEET

Date of Action	
Action ("Approved"/"Denied")	

Borrower Name	
Borrower Name	

Servicing Officer	
Analyst Name	

Approving Body	
(Or Co-approvers)	

Initials of Approvers: Approved Subject To:

_____   _____

_____   _____

_____   _____

_____   _____

_____   _____

_____   _____

_____   _____

_____   _____

_____   _____

FIGURE 7–2:   DOCUMENTATION REVIEW WORKSHEET FOR
                REAL ESTATE LOANS

DOCUMENT:	REQUIRED:	IN FILE:	COMMENTS:
General Information:			
Credit Report/References	_____	_____	_____
Partnership Agreement	_____	_____	_____
Verification of Corp. Legal Name	_____	_____	_____
Resolution to Borrow	_____	_____	_____
Resolution to Deposit	_____	_____	_____
Commitment Letter	_____	_____	_____
_____	_____	_____	_____
_____	_____	_____	_____
Loan Information:			
Copy of Note	_____	_____	_____
Loan Agreement	_____	_____	_____
Modification Agreement	_____	_____	_____
Guarantee	_____	_____	_____
Assignment of Life Insurance	_____	_____	_____
Annual Financial Statements	_____	_____	_____
Reliance Letter	_____	_____	_____
Interim Financial Statements	_____	_____	_____
Financial Statement Spreads	_____	_____	_____
Required Ratios	_____	_____	_____
Personal Financial Statements	_____	_____	_____
Business Tax Returns	_____	_____	_____
Personal Tax Returns	_____	_____	_____
Balance/Deposit Requirements	_____	_____	_____
_____	_____	_____	_____
_____	_____	_____	_____
Real Estate Collateral:			
ABI in Trust	_____	_____	_____
Trust Agreement	_____	_____	_____

FIGURE 7–2 (Continued)

DOCUMENT:	REQUIRED:	IN FILE:	COMMENTS:
Mortgage	_____	_____	_____
Assignment of R.E. Contract	_____	_____	_____
Lease/Rent Assignment	_____	_____	_____
Title Commitment	_____	_____	_____
Title Policy	_____	_____	_____
Appraisal	_____	_____	_____
Appraisal Engagement Letter	_____	_____	_____
Appraisal Review Form	_____	_____	_____
Survey	_____	_____	_____
Insurance	_____	_____	_____
Prior Liens	_____	_____	_____
Flood Documentation	_____	_____	_____
Rent Roll	_____	_____	_____
Lease	_____	_____	_____

Environmental Documentation:

Environmental Indemnification	_____	_____	_____
Environmental Screening Report	_____	_____	_____
Phase I Audit/Site Inspection	_____	_____	_____
Phase II Audit/Site Inspection	_____	_____	_____

Other Collateral/Fixtures:

Security Agreement	_____	_____	_____
Third Party Pledge/Hypothecation	_____	_____	_____
County Financing Statement	_____	_____	_____
State Financing Statement	_____	_____	_____
County Lien Search	_____	_____	_____
State Lien Search	_____	_____	_____
Insurance	_____	_____	_____
_____	_____	_____	_____
_____	_____	_____	_____

Completed by: _____   Date:_____

FIGURE 7–3: DOCUMENTATION REVIEW WORKSHEET FOR
LOANS SECURED BY BUSINESS ASSETS

DOCUMENT:	REQUIRED:	IN FILE:	COMMENTS:
General Information:			
Credit Report/References	_____	_____	_____
Partnership Agreement	_____	_____	_____
Verification of Corp. Legal Name	_____	_____	_____
Resolution to Borrow	_____	_____	_____
Resolution to Deposit	_____	_____	_____
Commitment Letter	_____	_____	_____
_____	_____	_____	_____
_____	_____	_____	_____
Loan Information:			
Copy of Note	_____	_____	_____
Loan Agreement	_____	_____	_____
Modification Agreement	_____	_____	_____
Guarantee	_____	_____	_____
Assignment of Life Insurance	_____	_____	_____
Annual Financial Statements	_____	_____	_____
Reliance Letter	_____	_____	_____
Interim Financial Statements	_____	_____	_____
Financial Statement Spreads	_____	_____	_____
Required Ratios	_____	_____	_____
Personal Financial Statements	_____	_____	_____
Business Tax Returns	_____	_____	_____
Personal Tax Returns	_____	_____	_____
Balance/Deposit Requirements	_____	_____	_____
_____	_____	_____	_____
_____	_____	_____	_____
Business Asset Collateral:			
Security Agreement	_____	_____	_____
County Financing Statement	_____	_____	_____

FIGURE 7–3 (Continued)

DOCUMENT:	REQUIRED:	IN FILE:	COMMENTS:
State Financing Statement	_____	_____	_____
County Lien Search	_____	_____	_____
State Lien Search	_____	_____	_____
Vehicle Title	_____	_____	_____
Power of Attorney	_____	_____	_____
Insurance	_____	_____	_____
Borrowing Base Certificates	_____	_____	_____
Equipment List	_____	_____	_____
Inventory List	_____	_____	_____
Accounts Receivable Aging	_____	_____	_____
Accounts Payable Aging	_____	_____	_____

Other Collateral:

Security Agreement	_____	_____	_____
Third Party Pledge/Hypothecation	_____	_____	_____
Mortgage	_____	_____	_____
ABI in Trust	_____	_____	_____
_____	_____	_____	_____
_____	_____	_____	_____

Completed by: _____   Date: _____

FIGURE 7–4: DOCUMENTATION REVIEW WORKSHEET FOR
              LOANS SECURED BY DEPOSITS OR SECURITIES

DOCUMENT:	REQUIRED:	IN FILE:	COMMENTS:
General Information:			
Credit Report/References	_____	_____	_____
Partnership Agreement	_____	_____	_____
Verification of Corp. Legal Name	_____	_____	_____
Resolution to Borrow	_____	_____	_____
Resolution to Deposit	_____	_____	_____
Commitment Letter	_____	_____	_____
_____	_____	_____	_____
_____	_____	_____	_____
Loan Information:			
Copy of Note	_____	_____	_____
Loan Agreement	_____	_____	_____
Modification Agreement	_____	_____	_____
Guarantee	_____	_____	_____
Assignment of Life Insurance	_____	_____	_____
Annual Financial Statements	_____	_____	_____
Reliance Letter	_____	_____	_____
Interim Financial Statements	_____	_____	_____
Financial Statement Spreads	_____	_____	_____
Required Ratios	_____	_____	_____
Personal Financial Statements	_____	_____	_____
Business Tax Returns	_____	_____	_____
Personal Tax Returns	_____	_____	_____
Balance/Deposit Requirements	_____	_____	_____
_____	_____	_____	_____
_____	_____	_____	_____
Negotiable Securities Collateral:			
Possession of Negotiable Security	_____	_____	_____
Stock or Bond Power	_____	_____	_____

FIGURE 7–4 (Continued)

DOCUMENT:	REQUIRED:	IN FILE:	COMMENTS:
Collateral Receipt	_____	_____	_____
Update of Current Market Value	_____	_____	_____

CD/Savings/Cash Value Life Ins:urance

Security Agreement	_____	_____	_____
CD/Sav. Acct. Endorsed to Bank	_____	_____	_____
Hold or Flag on Account	_____	_____	_____
Collateral Receipt	_____	_____	_____
Assignment/Cash Value of Life Insurance	_____	_____	_____

Other Collateral:

Security Agreement	_____	_____	_____
Third-Party Pledge/Hypothecation	_____	_____	_____
Mortgage	_____	_____	_____
ABI in Trust	_____	_____	_____
_____	_____	_____	_____
_____	_____	_____	_____

Completed by: _____   Date: _____

FIGURE 7–5: SAMPLE PRICING ANALYSIS FOR A COMMERCIAL RELATIONSHIP*

DATA INPUT BY THE ANALYST

Rate and Return Data for the Bank:

Bank prime spread from *The Wall Street Journal* prime:	0.00%
Floating cost of funds spread from bank prime:	3.00%
DDA earning allowance spread from bank prime:	4.00%
DDA reserve requirement:	10.00%
Money market earning allowance spread from bank prime:	5.00%
Cert. of deposit earning allowance spread from bank prime:	6.00%
Savings reserve requirement:	0.00%
Bank capital to asset ratio:	10.00%
Bank tax rate:	40.00%
Target return on loan assets (percent of loans, after tax):	2.50%
Target return on investment (after tax):	20.00%

Risk Rating Table for the Bank:

LOAN CLASSIFICATION	RISK ADD-ON	SERVICING ADD-ON
1. Pass (Grade 1)	0.00%	0.00%
2. Pass (Grade 2)	0.00%	0.00%
3. Pass (Grade 3)	0.25%	0.00%
4. Pass (Grade 4)	0.50%	0.25%
5. Watch List	1.50%	1.00%
6. OAEM	3.00%	3.00%
7. Substandard	15.00%	15.00%
8. Doubtful	50.00%	50.00%
9. Loss	100.00%	100.00%

*© American Bankers Association. Reprinted with permission. All Rights Reserved. For order inquiries, call 1-800-338-0626.

FIGURE 7–5 (Continued)

Relationship Information for the Customer:

Current *Wall Street Journal* prime:	6.75%
Relationship risk classification:	4
Annual account analysis earnings:	$0
Average account balance not on analysis:	$25,000
Money market deposits:	$1,000
Money market interest rate paid:	3.00%
Certificates of Deposit:	$10,000
Certificates of Deposit interest rate paid:	4.00%
Total fees and other income:	$1,000
Amount of loan:	$100,000
Amount of off-balance sheet debt for loan:	$0
Loan interest rate:	7.75%

DATA OUTPUT BY THE PROGRAM

Total funded debt:	$100,000	100.00%
Total off-balance sheet:	$0	0.00%
Interest income from loans:	$7,750	7.75%
Total earning allowance:	$780	0.78%
Fees and other income:	$1,000	1.00%
Gross interest and fee income:	$9,530	9.53%
Interest expense:	$430	0.43%
Cost of funds:	$3,750	3.75%
Net interest spread:	$5,350	5.35%
Risk provision:	$500	0.50%
Servicing:	$250	0.25%
Income tax expense:	$1,840	1.84%
Total Net Income/ROA:	$2,760	2.76%

FIGURE 7–5 (Continued)

Target ROA:	$2,500	2.50%
Over/under target ROA:	$260	**0.26%**
Return on equity (after tax):	$2,760	27.60%
Target ROA:	$2,000	20.00%
Over/under target ROE:	$760	**7.60%**

CHAPTER EIGHT

REGULATIONS AND COMPLIANCE

COMMUNITY REINVESTMENT ACT (CRA)

Background

The Community Reinvestment Act of 1977 (CRA) is a regulation requiring "each appropriate federal financial supervisory agency to use its authority when examining financial institutions, to encourage such institutions to help meet the credit needs of the local community in which they are chartered consistent with the safe and sound operation of such institutions" (*Community Reinvestment Act of 1977*).

In order to meet the requirements of CRA, the bank must make a special effort to lend to the middle and low income areas of its market. In addition, the bank must document its CRA efforts and results, and the bank must make the documentation available to anyone wishing to see it. The bank's regulating agency examines this documentation along with comments received from community members and bank management, and the agency rates the bank's compliance with CRA by assigning a grade of "Outstanding," "Satisfactory," "Needs to Improve," or "Substantial Noncompliance." These ratings are disclosed to the public, and they are considered, for example, when a bank requests permission from regulators to acquire another bank.

Support by the Credit Department

Credit department members can contribute to the bank's CRA effort by becoming aware of the provisions of the Act and by becoming familiar with some of the bank's efforts and successes in the CRA area. As a representative of the bank, each department member should be able to discuss the bank's CRA effort with customers and community members. Also, each department member should be aware of the area of the bank where the publicly accessible CRA file is located.

Also, any CRA implications should be discussed by the analyst in the loan presentation. It is, however, important to realize that while CRA requires special efforts to meet the needs of the middle and low-income market, credit standards and decision making should not be affected by CRA implications. A loan should be approved based on its own merits, regardless of CRA benefits.

An additional contribution that the department can make to the CRA effort is organization of the reporting of customer calls with CRA implications. Department members can collect reports of all CRA calls made by loan officers, and they can compile a log and reports of these activities.

NATIONAL FLOOD INSURANCE PROGRAM AND FLOOD DISASTER PROTECTION ACT

Background

The National Flood Insurance Program was instituted in 1968 as a result of significant flood damage in the United States. The purpose of the program (and the 1973 Flood Disaster Protection Act) is to make the public aware of the dangers of flooding, to define areas that are prone to flooding, and to promote floodplain management by communities.

In addition, the program offers to property owners flood insurance, which had previously been virtually unavailable. In fact, flood insurance is mandatory for mortgage loans on properties located in special flood hazard areas in communities that participate in the National Flood Insurance Program. All banks that are federally regulated or are members of the FDIC must notify prospective borrowers if their properties are located in special flood hazard areas, they must inform prospective borrowers whether federal disaster assistance is available, and they are also responsible for seeing that flood insurance (if available) is maintained for the term of the loan.

The Federal Emergency Management Agency (Washington, DC) and its regional offices provide details on the program including flood maps and lists of participating communities.

Support by the Credit Department

The credit department can support compliance with flood regulation in various ways. The credit department can store flood maps and be responsible for using them to determine whether properties are located in special flood hazard areas. Location of a collateral property in a flood hazard area can be discussed by the analyst in the collateral section of the loan presentation.

If loan documentation or documentation review is the responsibility of the Credit Analyst, then he or she can determine that the appropriate documentation is performed and stored in the credit file. Documentation includes evidence and date that a flood map was consulted, notification (if necessary) that a borrower is in a special flood hazard area including whether insurance is available, and proof of insurance (if required). Note that the real estate documentation review checklist in Chapter 7 includes flood documentation as a line item.

EQUAL CREDIT OPPORTUNITY ACT (REGULATION B)

Background

The Equal Credit Opportunity Act (Regulation B) took effect in 1977, and it applies to all credit (commercial and personal) regardless of type of credit or creditor. The Act states that financial institutions cannot discriminate against a loan applicant or discourage loan application on the basis of race, color, religion, national origin, sex, marital status, or age. Also, financial institutions generally cannot require information on race, color, religion, national origin, sex, marital status, age, outside support such as alimony or child support, or information on childrearing and childbearing.

The Act also states that, in general, financial institutions cannot require information on a spouse or former spouse, and financial institutions cannot require a spouse or other person to sign or apply jointly for a loan. However, if a spouse or other person benefits from a loan (for example, when the spouse also receives loan funds or uses the account), or if a spouse or other person provides support for a loan (for example, when the spouse provides income or collateral), then these rules do not apply.

Finally, the Act states that, in general, formal notice of adverse action (denial of a requested loan) must be made within 30 days, and that notice of adverse action must include reasons for denial.

Further information on the Equal Credit Opportunity Act can be obtained from the Federal Reserve Bank of your bank's district or from your bank's regulating agency.

Support by the Credit Department

Credit department members should support compliance with the Equal Credit Opportunity Act by reporting any discriminatory or potentially discriminatory practices to their supervisor or by reporting them in loan analyses. For example, requiring a spouse's personal guarantee when the spouse has no ownership interest in the business potentially violates the Equal Credit Opportunity Act. If the spouse does not benefit from the loan, and if the spouse does not provide financial support or collateral for the loan, then it is likely that requiring the personal guarantee violates Regulation B. This potential violation should be noted clearly by the analyst in the loan presentation.

The credit department can also be responsible for tracking written notices of adverse action. Department members can track commercial loan applications, complete adverse action notices, send them within the required time periods, and file them appropriately.

TITLE XI OF FIRREA

Background

Title XI of the Financial Institutions Reform, Recovery, and Enforcement Act of 1989 (FIRREA) addresses real estate appraisals. According to the provisions of Title XI of FIRREA, "The purpose of this title is to provide that federal financial and public policy interests in real estate related transactions will be protected by requiring that real estate appraisals utilized in connection with federally related transactions are performed in writing, in accordance with uniform standards, by individuals whose competency has been demonstrated and whose professional conduct will be subject to effective supervision."

In other words, financial institutions are required to support real estate transactions with written appraisals performed according to uniform standards by appraisers who satisfy certain criteria. The regulation states that appraisals will be performed according to the Uniform Standards of Professional Appraisal Practice (USPAP). This provides uniformity and accuracy in appraising.

To administer the regulation, each state certifies and licenses appraisers and prepares listings of such appraisers. State-licensed appraisers are required for all transactions over $250,000, and state-certified appraisers are required for all complex or nonresidential transactions and for all transactions over $1 million.

Title XI of FIRREA and its interpretation by regulating agencies requires that all real estate transactions over $250,000 be supported by an appraisal with the following exceptions (OCC Bulletin 94-37, 1994):

- When a lien on real estate is taken as an "abundance of caution." The bank must document that the loan is supported by other income or collateral and that the real estate is being taken as additional collateral to use this exception.

- When a loan is not secured by real estate.

- When a lien on real estate is taken for purposes other than the real estate's value. For example, when the lien provides the bank control over and access to non-real estate collateral, which may include the business operating as a going concern.

- When a commercial loan has a transaction value of less than $1 million and the loan is not dependent on the sale of or rental income from the property as the primary source of repayment.

■ When a transaction consists of an operating lease that is not the economic equivalent of a purchase or sale of the real estate.

■ When a loan is renewed with no new funds provided, when the borrower has performed satisfactorily, and when the property has not deteriorated.

■ When an institution purchases or participates in a loan transaction.

■ When a loan is insured or guaranteed by the U.S. government or when the loan meets all of the qualifications for sale to a U.S. government agency or government-sponsored agency such as Fannie Mae, Farmer Mac, or Freddie Mac.

■ When the bank is acting solely in a fiduciary capacity (such as the Trust Department) and is not required to obtain an appraisal under other law.

■ When the regulating agency determines that the services of an appraiser are not necessary.

The regulation also states that, in general, the bank must **engage the appraiser directly** and the appraiser shall have no interest, direct or indirect, in the property or the transaction. To comply with this requirement, the bank should order appraisals in writing through a standard "engagement letter." This action ensures that the appraiser is aware of the bank's regulatory requirements, and it documents the fact that the bank ordered the appraisal. When received, the appraisal should note that it has been performed for the bank. Note that the regulation does, however, permit the bank to accept appraisals prepared by or prepared for other financial institutions.

Further details on Title XI of FIRREA and its interpretation can be obtained from your bank's regulating agency. Copies or information regarding the Uniform Standards of Professional Appraisal Practice can be obtained from:

The Appraisal Foundation
1029 Vermont Avenue, N.W., Suite 900
Washington, DC 20005-3517
Phone: (202) 347-7722
Fax: (202) 347-7727

Support by the Credit Department

The credit department can support compliance with FIRREA in two important ways. First, the department can maintain a list of state-certified and state-licensed appraisers who are approved for use by the bank. Department members can ensure that all appraisals are performed by state-certified or state-licensed appraisers when required by the regulation. Department members can also ensure that engagement letters are used and that appraisals are written for the bank. Compliance or noncompliance should be noted in the loan presentation as well as on the loan documentation review forms.

The second way that the department can support compliance with FIRREA is to review finished appraisals. Appraisals should be reviewed for quality and for conformance with the Uniform Standards of Professional Appraisal Practice. Figure 8–1, a sample appraisal review form, appears at the end of this chapter.[1]

ENVIRONMENTAL LEGISLATION

Background

Legislation such as the Comprehensive Environmental Response, Compensation, and Liability Act of 1980 (CERCLA) and the Superfund Amendments and Reauthorization Act of 1986 (SARA) requires clean-up of environmentally contaminated real estate. This legislation, along with the continuing trend in recognition of environmental contamination, affects banks in various ways.

Most importantly, when a borrower's real estate (regardless of whether the bank has a lien on the property) is contaminated, clean-up and/or litigation costs inhibit the borrower's ability to repay bank debt. Additionally, if the bank does have a lien on the contaminated real estate, the bank's collateral position deteriorates. Finally, if the bank ever owns or operates a contaminated real estate property, the bank may become liable for clean-up costs.

---

1 This form was prepared by Michael T. White, a loan review officer at First Midwest Bank and a former bank examiner.

Support by the Credit Department

In order to mitigate this risk, banks require environmental documentation and perform analysis to determine the existence of environmental hazards when lending to commercial borrowers. The credit department can participate in this process.

Credit department members can be responsible for ensuring that environmental documentation is received and filed properly. Environmental documentation is included in the Documentation Review Checklist in Chapter 7. In addition, department members can examine the documentation for the existence of or potential for environmental hazards. This analysis should be contained in every loan presentation.

Banks typically require completion of an indemnity agreement and an environmental checklist and/or screening for every commercial loan. A checklist is typically completed by the loan officer as he or she examines the site. An environmental screening is a report that details government registered environmental hazards on the site and nearby. Companies such as Vista Environmental Information, Inc. [5060 Shorham Place, Suite 300, San Diego, California 92122; (619) 450-6100] provide environmental screenings and title searches for environmental purposes at relatively inexpensive prices.

In addition, a clear Phase I environmental audit is typically required for all loans over a certain dollar amount. A Phase I is an expert analysis and opinion of the possibility of environmental hazards; it includes an environmental screening and a site visit by the auditor. Finally, a clear Phase II environmental audit (consisting of actual samples of the parcel) is typically required whenever an environmental screening or a Phase I reveals the potential existence of any environmental hazards.

SOURCES

Community Reinvestment Act of 1977. Pub. L. 95–128, title VIII, Section 802, October 12, 1977, 91 Stat. 1147 & Stat. 1148.

1991 Comptroller's Manual for National Banks: Volume I— Laws. (Washington, DC.: Comptroller of the Currency).

Financial Institutions Reform, Recovery, and Enforcement Act of 1989. Title XI.

Mortgage Lenders Workshop: National Flood Insurance Program Participant Manual. (Federal Emergency Management Agency, 1987).

N.A. Loan Policy: Environmental Policy and Procedures Manual. First Midwest Bank/Danville (November 2, 1993).

OCC Bulletin 94–37. (Washington, D.C.: Comptroller of the Currency, June 7, 1994).

Official Staff Commentary on Regulation B Equal Credit Opportunity. (Board of Governors of the Federal Reserve System, rev. August 1992).

Rayburn, William B. and Tosh, Dennis S. *Banker's Real Estate Appraisal Compliance Manual* (Austin, Texas: Sheshunoff Information Services, Inc., 1994).

Regulation B Equal Credit Opportunity. (Board of Governors of the Federal Reserve System, rev. August 1992).

FIGURE 8–1: SAMPLE APPRAISAL REVIEW FORM

Borrower Name: _____

Property Address: _____

Appraiser Name: _____

APPRAISAL FEATURE	YES	NO	COMMENTS
General Observations:			
Appraiser approved	_____	_____	_____
Report is complete	_____	_____	_____
Photographs adequate	_____	_____	_____
Maps adequate	_____	_____	_____
Sketches adequate	_____	_____	_____
Report dated	_____	_____	_____
Report signed	_____	_____	_____
Identifications:			
Address provided	_____	_____	_____
Legal description provided	_____	_____	_____
Neighborhood:			
Adequate description	_____	_____	_____
Marketing time provided	_____	_____	_____
Marketing time over 6 months	_____	_____	_____
Explanation if over 6 months	_____	_____	_____

FIGURE 8–1 (Continued)

	YES	NO	COMMENTS
Subject Property:			
Age provided	_____	_____	_____
Type of construction provided	_____	_____	_____
Size of property provided	_____	_____	_____
Size consistent with market value	_____	_____	_____
Improvements:			
Comments on physical condition	_____	_____	_____
Comments on age, construction utility, size, equipment	_____	_____	_____
Comments on structural problems, settling, wetness	_____	_____	_____
Comments on marketability	_____	_____	_____
Highest and Best Use Analysis:			
Land use regulations (zoning)	_____	_____	_____
Market demand	_____	_____	_____
Physical adaptability	_____	_____	_____
Neighborhood trends	_____	_____	_____
Optimum or alternative uses	_____	_____	_____
Anticipated public projects	_____	_____	_____
Outside feasibility studies	_____	_____	_____

FIGURE 8–1 (Continued)

	YES	NO	COMMENTS

Market Comparable Analysis:

Comparables have same
highest and best use   _____ _____ _____

Comparables physically and
economically similar   _____ _____ _____

Comparables appear appropriate _____ _____ _____

Reasonable sales valuation   _____ _____ _____

Cost Approach:

Cost figures appropriate for
market   _____ _____ _____

Depreciation figures reasonable _____ _____ _____

Land value estimate reasonable _____ _____ _____

Reasonable cost valuation   _____ _____ _____

Income Approach:

Income, expense, vacancy
information current/accurate   _____ _____ _____

Cap rate is used   _____ _____ _____

Cap rate is reasonable   _____ _____ _____

Income valuation appears
logical   _____ _____ _____

FIGURE 8–1 (Continued)

	YES	NO	COMMENTS
Requirements Met:			
Engagement letter attached	_____	_____	_____
Engagement letter complete	_____	_____	_____
Report satisfies USPAP requirements	_____	_____	_____

Explain any unmet requirements:

_____

_____

Reviewer concurrence or disagreement with value reached:

_____

_____

Comments:

_____

_____

Reviewer Signature:_____   Date: _____

SUMMARY

The successful credit department manager performs a wide variety of functions. He or she must be a leader, a planner, a communicator, an organizer, a teacher, and an analyst. The credit department manager who leads the creation or the ongoing operation of the credit department must possess each of these skills. The credit manager position is, therefore, one of great responsibility and challenge.

The credit department manager leads an ongoing, step-by-step process as the head of the credit department. This process begins with goal setting and planning, and it proceeds with department structuring or restructuring and staffing. The department manager sees that the operation of the department is characterized by the appropriate levels of organization and communication. The department manager is also responsible for ensuring that department goals and objectives are achieved through its operations. Effective training and motivation help goals to become achieved, and an incentive program reinforces the appropriate behaviors in department members.

The following list represents a guide and an example of the typical operation of the commercial loan analysis process. This list brings together the tasks and the operational forms presented throughout this book:

1. A loan officer brings a customer's file and a recently received financial statement to one of the credit analysts. The loan officer mentions that the customer would like to make an asset purchase to be financed by the bank. The officer asks the analyst to spread the updated financial statement and to provide a preliminary feasibility analysis of the asset purchase along with any questions regarding the proposed transaction.

2. The analyst logs in the officer's analysis request on the department log-in form (Chapter 2), noting that the loan officer would like a **spread update** and a **debt service coverage analysis**.

3. After this particular request becomes the highest priority on the log-in list, one of the analysts puts the **date** and her **initials** next to the request on the log-in form to signify that she has begun to work on it. She uses a computer spreadsheet program (Chapter 2) to complete the spread.

4. When the analyst is finished, she notes the **date completed** and estimates the **hours used to complete the analysis** on the log-in form. She returns the file, the financial statement spread, and the debt service coverage analysis with questions to the loan officer. The

analyst also includes a blank "loan officer request form" (Chapter 2) with the information. This is included so that when the loan officer requests a full loan presentation, the analyst will begin to work with as much information as possible.

5.   After looking over the initial analysis, the loan officer decides to proceed with the loan request. The loan officer completes the loan officer request form with all of the necessary information and returns it, along with the file, to the credit department.

6.   The analyst who receives the file and the request form logs in the request for the loan presentation, noting the **type** of request and the **dollar amount** of the loan relationship for prioritization.

7.   After this request becomes the highest priority on the list, one of the analysts **initials** and **dates** the log-in form and begins to work on it.

8.   In addition to the conventional information, the analyst sends for a publication about the borrower's industry (Chapter 3) and performs a loan pricing analysis (Chapter 7). This information is included in the loan write-up.

9.   Once the loan presentation is nearly complete, the analyst presents it to the loan officer in draft form in order to get some details correct. The analyst also informs the loan officer that an updated personal financial statement on the principal will be necessary to complete the analysis.

10. The loan officer returns the draft with comments and with the necessary statement. When the draft is complete, the analyst reviews it using the loan presentation checklist (Chapter 3).

11. After the analyst has reviewed the presentation, each of the other credit department members receives a copy of the draft.

12. The morning before the next loan committee meeting, the department meets as a group to discuss the loan write-ups that will be presented to the committee the following day.

13. During the afternoon preceding the loan committee meeting, the analyst performs the final revisions to the presentation and distributes the final drafts of the presentation to each loan committee member.

14. The analyst notes the date completed and the time taken to complete the loan write-up on the log-in form.

15. The analyst attends the loan committee meeting the following day and answers a few questions that the committee has about the analysis.

16. The loan committee decides to approve the loan. The analyst passes a loan approval form (Chapter 7) around to each committee member for initials.

17. After the committee meeting, the analyst presents the loan approval form, the file, and a copy of the loan presentation to loan operations so that the documents can be prepared.

18. After the loan is closed, the analyst files all of the documents in the loan file and returns it to the proper place. In addition, the analyst notes the date that the loan matures and the date that the next review is required by loan policy on a tickler system (Chapter 7).

The next list represents the typical day of a credit department manager. The credit department manager performs a wide variety of tasks, and he or she has a great deal of responsibilities:

1. On your way into the Credit Department in the morning, a loan assistant asks for help with her computer.

2. After you hang up your coat and get a cup of coffee, an analyst asks you a few questions about a loan presentation that she has nearly completed.

3. At 9:00 A.M. you attend a meeting of the bank's loan policy committee. You suggest ways that your department can assist the commercial lenders with compliance with policy, and you take notes on approved changes to the policy.

4. You leave the loan policy meeting early to attend an 11:00 A.M. call on a borrower in a workout situation. You suggest plans to the loan officer for improving the loan relationship, and you act as a witness at the meeting.

5. When you return to the bank, you meet the Senior lender for lunch. He updates you about the discussion in the loan policy committee meeting, which occurred after you left. You discuss ways to improve the credit

department's relationship with the commercial lenders and support of the commercial lending function.

6. When you return from lunch, you meet with the department to discuss the loan presentations for the following day's loan committee meeting. You also discuss plans for assisting the lenders in compliance with loan policy and changes in loan policy approved at the morning meeting.

7. After the department meeting, you spread a financial statement for a loan presentation, which an analyst must finish in a hurry in order to be ready for the loan committee meeting the following day.

8. You return to your desk and read the day's mail.

9. After reading the mail, you read each of the loan presentations for the committee meeting in detail. This prompts you to suggest some minor improvements to the analysts.

10. While discussing a presentation with one of the analysts, he asks about his benefits. You describe his benefits and answer his questions.

11. Next, a loan officer approaches you to ask your advice about restructuring a small loan to a new business.

12. The bank president then calls to request loan reports that were completed recently. You ask the analyst who prepares the reports to make copies and distribute them to the president and to each of the loan officers.

13. When you return to your desk, the bank president calls with questions about the reports, which he has just received.

14. After meeting with the president to discuss the reports and the loan presentations for the following day's meeting, it is 6:30 P.M. You pack up and go home for the evening.

The credit department performs a crucial bank function, and the credit department manager has a vital role in the management of the bank. Objective loan analysis and support and control of the commercial lending function are extremely important, and your bank's success depends in large measure on your success and that of the credit department.

I hope this manual will help you to operate a successful credit department, and I hope that your department will substantially contribute to your bank's success.

GLOSSARY

Accrual-Basis Cash Flow: An analysis of cash flow and ability to service debt that is based on the income statement and debt payments.

Advance Formula: Advance formulas are mathematical formulas that determine the amount of funds the bank will lend. For example, at any one time, the bank may be willing to lend up to 75 percent of accounts receivable less than 90 days plus, 50 percent of inventory, less work in process (Pirok 1994, 98).

Amortization: Amortization is the length of time over which loan payments are spread. An amortization schedule details regular payment and remaining balance amounts over the life of a loan.

Analyst: *See* "Credit Analyst."

Appraisal: A written estimate of the value of a real estate property.

Assignment: An assignment allows some payment due to a borrower to be made directly to the bank in the event of default by the borrower. For example, rent payments from tenants may be paid directly to the bank if the borrower defaults on a mortgage or if the bank takes ownership or control of the property. In addition to rent or lease streams, any present or future source of cash can be specifically assigned to the bank. This includes payments on accounts or notes receivable, tax refunds, insurance refunds, life insurance proceeds, interests in a trust, or even lottery winnings (Pirok 1994, 100).

Audited Financial Statements: Audited financial statements result when the accountant strictly examines the financial statements. Account balances including loans, deposits, receivables, payables, and inventory are audited. The auditor also gives an opinion on the ability of the firm to continue as a going-concern (Pirok 1994, 6).

Balloon: *See* "Term."

Bank Examination: A regular examination or audit made by a bank's regulating agency. Bank examinations are performed to determine safety, soundness, and compliance with regulations.

Borrowing Base Certificate: A form filled out regularly by a borrower to update the bank regarding current collateral amounts. The use of a borrowing base certificate ensures the bank that funds are advanced against sufficient collateral amounts.

Breakeven Analysis: Determination of a revenue amount or an amount of units that must be sold to service expense and debt requirements and provide no additional cash flow.

Business Assets: Business assets include accounts, accounts receivable, fixed assets such as machinery and equipment, inventory, and intangibles. Business assets exclude real estate. Business assets are assigned to the bank as collateral through a security agreement and a financing statement or UCC filing (Pirok 1994, 100).

Business Plan: A business plan is a description of an organization and its strategies and operations. Business plans typically address SWOT analysis, competition, products, R&D, pricing, marketing, and management.

Cash-Basis Cash Flow: An analysis of cash flow and ability to service debt based on the statement of cash flows and debt requirements.

Cash Flow Analysis: An analysis of cash flow and/or debt service ability. Cash flow is measured by actual inflows and outflows and excludes noncash expenses such as depreciation. *See* Accrual-Basis Cash Flow and Cash-Basis Cash Flow.

Clean-Up Period: A clean-up period is a period of time where the borrower must maintain a zero loan balance. The bank will typically require a 60-day clean-up period annually on a revolving line of credit (Pirok 1994, 104).

Coercive Power: Power derived from the ability to punish others.

Collateral: Collateral or security is an asset or assets that are pledged by a borrower to a lender to induce a loan. If the borrower defaults on the loan, then the lender has the right to assume ownership of the collateral.

Commercial Lending Department: The bank department comprised of loan officers and their assistants and support staff. Commercial loan officers sell and administer commercial loans. Loan officers request analysis and other supporting work from the credit department.

Commitment Letter: A letter that, when signed by a representative of the bank and the borrower, commits the bank to lend and the borrower to borrow. The letter typically details all relevant terms of the loan.

Community Reinvestment Act: The Community Reinvestment Act (CRA) is a regulation stating that the bank must make a special effort to lend to the middle and low-income areas of its market. In addition, the bank must document this effort and the results and make the documentation available to anyone who wishes to see it.

Compiled Financial Statements: Compiled statements are CPA prepared, but the accountant makes no opinion as to the accuracy of the statements (Pirok 1994, 6).

CRA: *See* "Community Reinvestment Act."

Credit Administration Department: A commercial credit department that has loan administration, documentation, and operation responsibilities in addition to commercial loan analysis responsibility. *See also* "Credit Department."

Credit Analyst: A credit department member whose primary responsibility is to analyze commercial loans.

Credit Department: The credit department (or "credit administration department," "credit analysis department," or "commercial loan analysis department") is responsible for both supporting and controlling the commercial lending department in various ways. The Credit Department's primary activity is generally analysis of commercial loans.

Credit Inquiry: An inquiry made regarding the credit history of a commercial borrower of the bank. Banks frequently exchange credit information with other banks and with trade creditors of commercial borrowers. For example, a supplier of a commercial borrower may inquire about the borrower's repayment history to the bank to determine whether it wishes to supply its product to the borrower on credit.

Credit File: A file containing all relevant information and documents for a loan customer.

Customer Call: A meeting between one or more representatives of the bank and one or more representatives of a bank client or prospective client. The customer call generally takes place at the customer's place of business, and its purpose may be selling or prospecting, informational, receipt of loan request details, or for problem-solving purposes.

Deed in Trust: An agreement used in some states instead of a mortgage to pledge real estate as collateral. Using a deed in trust, the lender holds the title to the property until the loan is paid in full.

Equal Credit Opportunity Act: The Equal Credit Opportunity Act (ECOA or Regulation B) states that financial institutions cannot discriminate against a loan applicant or discourage loan application on the basis of race, color, religion, national origin, sex, marital status, or age.

Examination: *See* "Bank Examination."

Expert Power: Power derived from experience and knowledge.

Expiration: *See* "Term."

File Clerk: Someone responsible for tracking, spreading, and organizing financial statements.

Financial Statements: Reports such as income statements, balance sheets, statements of cash flow, and reconciliations of retained earnings that detail financial aspects of a business or individual.

Financing Statement: A statement (such as a UCC-1 or a UCC-3) filed with a state or local government to detail business assets and to take the assets as collateral.

FIRREA: *See* "Title XI of FIRREA."

Flood and Flood Insurance: *See* "National Flood Insurance Program."

Guarantee: A guarantee occurs when a third party agrees to repay debt if the borrower defaults. For example, company owners are frequently required by the bank to personally guarantee repayment of loans made to the company. In addition, corporations frequently guarantee loans made to company owners or to related companies (Pirok 1994, 102–103).

Incentive: A reward offered to bring about a certain behavior.

Leadership: The ability to influence, persuade, and motivate others toward a certain end.

Legal Lending Limit: The maximum amount that a bank is allowed by law to lend to any given loan borrower or relationship.

Lien Search: A search of state or local government records that reveals all liens against an entity. The bank uses lien searches to determine that its liens are recorded properly.

Loan Agreement: A written agreement that details all terms and conditions of a loan. A loan agreement is typically used to detail any complex or important terms of a loan.

Loan Committee: A group of bank employees (typically commercial lenders) that has the authority to approve or deny loans (usually larger loan relationships), to set or recommend loan policy, and/or to approve or recommend loan risk ratings.

Loan Officer: An officer who is a member of the commercial lending department. Loan officers sell and administer commercial loans.

Loan Presentation: The loan presentation is the written report that the loan officer or committee uses to make a loan decision.

Loan to Value Ratio: The loan to value ratio is the ratio of one or more loan balances (or loan commitments) divided by the value of the collateral of the loan(s) (Pirok 1994, 101–102).

Loan Write-Up: *See* "Loan Presentation."

Log-In Form: A form used to "log in" each item of analysis work that is requested to be performed by the credit department. The log-in form is used for prioritization and tracking of analysis work, measurement of adherence to deadlines, and assignment of work to appropriate individuals.

Management Succession: Individuals who will take the place of current management in the event of their retirement, death, or inability to run the business.

Maturity: *See* "Term."

Mission: An organization's primary goal or function.

Modification Agreement: An agreement between the bank and a borrower that modifies the terms of an existing loan.

Mortgage: A mortgage is the means by which the bank takes real estate as collateral. The first mortgage holder has the first right (before the second mortgage holder and before any other creditors) of repayment from funds gained through liquidation of the real estate. The second mortgage holder has the right of repayment after the first mortgage holder has been repaid. A second mortgage holder may force liquidation of collateral, but it must pay the first mortgage holder in full before receiving any funds (Pirok 1994, 99).

National Flood Insurance Program: The National Flood Insurance Program (NFIP) was instituted to make the public aware of the dangers of flooding, to define areas that are prone to flooding, and to promote floodplain management by communities.

Obligor: A borrower or someone who signs a note, therefore becoming liable to repay the debt.

Personality Power: Power resulting from personality traits such as enthusiasm and persuasive ability.

Phase I Environmental Audit: An expert analysis and opinion of the possibility of environmental hazards for a real estate property. A clear Phase I is typically required for all commercial loans over a certain dollar amount.

Phase II Environmental Audit: A Phase II consists of actual environmental sampling of a real estate property. A clear Phase II is typically required whenever a Phase I reveals the potential existence of any environmental hazards.

Profitability Analysis: *See* "Relationship Profitability Analysis."

Regulation B: *See* "Equal Credit Opportunity Act."

Relationship Profitability Analysis: This process involves collecting bank-specific data and goals and measuring whether each individual commercial customer is profitable to the bank. The use of profitability analysis is also a tool for the pricing of proposed loans.

Reliance Letter: A letter from an accountant of a bank customer to the bank that allows the bank to rely on and hold the accountant liable for the figures presented in the financial statements.

Resolution: A corporate resolution results when a company's board of directors meets and authorizes certain officers to borrow or deposit funds in the name of the company. A written resolution is required in order for a company to borrow from the bank.

Reviewed Financial Statements: Reviewed statements are examined for accuracy by the accountant, but the examination is significantly less in scope than an audit (Pirok 1994, 6).

Reward Power: Power derived from the right to provide positive reinforcement or to reward others.

Risk Rating: A value assigned to a loan or loan relationship that represents the amount of risk to the bank that is inherent in the loan or loans. Credit Analysts typically recommend loan risk ratings as a part of the analysis process.

Security: *See* "Collateral."

Security Agreement: An agreement between the borrower and the bank allowing the bank to take business assets as collateral.

Spreadsheet Program: A computer program used to analyze financial statements. Balance sheet and income statement values from statements provided by the commercial borrower are input by the analyst. The program then produces detailed financial statements for multiple years presented side by side. The output includes percentages of total assets or total sales, various financial ratios, reconciliations, and cash flow statements.

Statement of Cash Flows: A financial statement that presents actual cash flows as opposed to the accrual basis figures of the income statement. The statement of cash flows is a combination of the income statement and the balance sheet, and it is an important tool for commercial loan analysis.

Survey: A map of a plot of real estate detailing the boundaries of the property as well as easements or other encumbrances to the property.

Term: A loan's term, maturity, expiration, or balloon refers to its duration or to the time at which the loan commitment ends. The remaining principal and all accrued interest are due at this time. Upon maturity, the loan is typically reviewed by both the bank and the borrower. Either party may decide not to renew the loan after it has expired (Pirok 1994, 98).

Tickler System: A computer program or spreadsheet used to alert the user of due dates. A tickler system can be used to alert the bank to financial statements, insurance renewals, or UCC filing renewals that need to be acted on.

Title Commitment/Title Policy: The bank typically uses title insurance for all real estate transactions. A title company searches for all liens, easements, and other encumbrances to a real estate property prior to its purchase and issues a title policy commitment subject to the listed encumbrances. The title policy goes into effect when the borrower purchases the real estate. The policy insures the bank against any subsequent claims that the borrower may not rightfully own the real estate (subject to the original listed encumbrances).

Title XI of FIRREA: Title XI of the Financial Institutions Reform, Recovery, and Enforcement Act of 1989 (FIRREA) addresses real estate appraisals. According to the provisions of Title XI of FIRREA, "The purpose of this title is to provide that federal financial and public policy interests in real estate related transactions will be protected by requiring that real estate appraisals utilized in connection with federally related transactions are performed in writing, in accordance with uniform standards, by individuals whose competency has been demonstrated and whose professional conduct will be subject to effective supervision."

Traditional Cash Flow: *See* "Accrual-Basis Cash Flow."

Working Capital: Excess of current assets such as receivables and inventory over current liabilities (those due within one year).

SOURCES

Daft, Richard L. *Management* (Chicago: The Dryden Press, 1988), 366–424.

Financial Institutions Reform, Recovery, and Enforcement Act of 1989. Title XI.

Matz, Leonard M. *Self-Paced Documentation Training* (Austin, Texas: Sheshunoff Information Services, Inc., 1993).

Pirok, Kenneth R. *Commercial Loan Analysis* (Chicago: Probus Publishing Company, 1994).

Robbins, Stephen P. *Organizational Behavior* (Englewood Cliffs, New Jersey: Prentice Hall, 1989), 301–363.

INDEX

About the Author

Kenneth R. Pirok currently resides in Champaign, Illinois, where he operates a consulting business for banks and small businesses. He concentrates on loan and investment analysis as well as helping small businesses obtain financing.

He graduated from the University of Illinois with a Bachelor of Science degree in Finance. He has been a credit analyst at First Midwest Bank in Danville, Illinois and First of America Bank in Libertyville, Illinois. He recently played an instrumental role in the reorganization of a credit department, and he has also been responsible for providing analysis training to lenders and analysts.

Mr. Pirok has written lending books entitled *Commercial Loan Analysis* (Probus, 1994) and *The Lender's Toolkit* (Irwin Professional Publishing, 1995), and he wrote an article about the use of committees for commercial lending decisions which appeared in the February 1993 *Journal of Commercial Lending*. His plans for the future include pursuit of an MBA degree as well as more business, banking, and real estate books.